AUTHOR'S NOTE

Some friends consented to the publication of their real names in A Long Way to Life. However, some people's names have been changed to protect their anonymity, including relatives both living and deceased. Specifically worth noting is the name change of the character represented as "Mother."

DEDICATION

To my sons, I want to thank you for giving me a reason to live. To my dearest friend, Peggy, you have always been there for me. You have been my inspiration. To the children out there who have been in foster care or abused in some way, know that there is help out there. Just follow that light at the end of the path.

H ere are a few of my friends that wanted to share their thoughts and feelings about me.

The year was 1990 when, as a Birthright volunteer, I first met Nancy. She was twenty-five years old and pregnant with her second child. We talked, and talked. As she shared what was going on in her life, our friendship began and has continued to this day. I have always been impressed with Nancy's ability to persevere and resolve problems, find resources and mostly triumph's over any adversity in her life. It was so difficult to raise three children without much of a support system. But through the years, Nancy has always tried to grow and become a better person. Wishing Nancy all the best with this new venture.

Love Peg

I have known Nancy for two years. She started volunteering at the nursing home I'm in. I think Nancy is very considerate and kind, especially to old people.

Emily

I first met Nancy back in elementary school. Nancy is a very sweet and kind women. We stayed in touch throughout school. After graduation we lost contact. I always wondered what happened to her. After thirty some odd years later I found her on social media. I am so happy we did because we are good friends, and we help each other through difficult times.

Dave

I have never met anybody with such a warm heart. Nancy cares about everybody with problems. She gives advice physically and mentally. She has a heart of gold. I am proud to be one of her friends.

Rosali

CONTENTS

CHAPTER 1

AGE FIVE TO GRADE SCHOOL

I t was a bright, luminous day in 1969. My family and I were living in an apartment in Bayside Queens, New York. This was where my first horrific memory was created. I was five years old, shy and naive. My sister and I were fighting over a toy watch. My sister was two years younger than me. "Mother" was yelling from the bathroom that we should stop arguing. We continued, and again I heard that scarecrow voice. Now "Mother" was standing in the hallway, swinging a brush back and forth. It was a brush made of glass or something. As I watched, the brush began spiraling out of control, flying straight for me. I froze, and

I felt a hard hit. I put my hand to my head and saw blood. She had aimed that brush at me. "Mother" got upset because she realized what she had done. She called my father at work, and we met at the hospital. I kept telling the doctor that my mommy cracked my head open. By the look in her eyes, I thought she was going to kill me. I was always afraid of her. "Mother" reminded me of the movie Mommy Dearest.

Back then, no one did anything when you said that someone was hurting you. Today, abuse is everywhere, and things are being done about it. Anyway, the doctor put a butterfly patch on my head. I had no idea what a butterfly patch was. I went home and told all my friends about what "Mother" did to me. I had a really nice friend—I wish I could remember her name—and we played together all the time. We went to Alexander Graham Bell School together.

Many of these incidents happened throughout my life. My memory is vague; I just remember bits and pieces. I still have horrible memories sealed away in my mind. My therapist tells me they are too painful to remember. She says I suppressed them somewhere in the back of my head.

We were still living in Bayside when someone broke a glass. I was told to throw it in the garbage bag, so I did what I was told. Later, my sister walked on the garbage bag that was lying on the floor and cut her foot on the broken glass. Of course it was my fault she got hurt. My parents started screaming at me. It was purely accidental, but they made me feel like a monster. There was another time when my dad got mad at me for something and pushed me, and I fell into the coffee table and got a fat lip. Another time, "Mother" and cousins were all sitting on my grandfather's stoop. I don't know why, but for some reason Mother pushed me off, and I fractured my collarbone.

As a young child, I felt taunted by "Mother." No child should have to feel this way about her own flesh and blood. As far as I can remember, she never really loved me. I never felt that we had a bond, because we didn't. I couldn't begin to tell you why. I couldn't understand why she would do the things she did to me. I only had recollections of more situations.

In 1971, when I was eight, I remember moving into a new house, in Elmont, New York. My sister and I had to share a room. We weren't close at all, and we didn't share any common interests. We did our own thing. She seemed to be close to "Mother" because she never got into trouble. I found out we lived around the corner from my grandfather, aunt, and uncle. I was told my grandmother had died before I was born of stomach cancer. That is why I was named Agnes Nancy, because "Mother" wanted her firstborn to be named after her mother. It was the ugliest name. They called me Nancy from the day I was born, which was stupid.

I didn't hear nice things about my grandmother. "Mother" used to tell me stories. One day she got punished and had to kneel on rice or something. Another time she said her mother could see the candy store from her window. She saw "Mother" standing outside it wearing something she did not like and told her to get home. She was wearing what they called back then peg pants, and she had some light lipstick on. She was hanging around all the boys, and she got the belt. Those are the only two stories she told me about my grandmother. Nothing nice. The funny thing is that same candy store was still there when I went to elementary school. One piece of candy cost a penny today that same piece of candy cost $1.00. But I never understood why "Mother" would beat one child and not the other.

My grandfather also wasn't the nicest man. He was a real Italian. He would call me stupid all the time. My grandfather owned his own bakery in Elmont, New York. I loved going there because I could eat all the cannoli cream. He would bring us fresh bread at five o'clock in the morning; we would have coffee with bread and butter and dunk the bread in the coffee. He made the most wonderful bread. But one morning, while driving to our house, he found a dog in the middle of the road and brought it home to us. "Mother" named him Surprise, because he was a surprise. He was a poodle that needed cleaning up. "Mother" took it to a vet and got his hair cut. He was also blind in one eye, which was sad. That dog wanted nothing to do with anyone but "Mother"; he followed her everywhere. She was nicer to the animals than she was to her daughter.

One day "Mother" had to go to work, and grandfather had to watch me. I was home sick with a fever. Grandpa wasn't paying attention, and I climbed on the counter and swallowed all the baby aspirins. When he finally realized what I did, he called "Mother." She came home, and they took me to the hospital, where they had to pump my stomach. I guess I wanted to kill myself then.

Grandpa treated my sister and me better than all of my other cousins. I don't know why he treated all of us differently. Every other Friday night, my sister and I would spend the night. He would buy us all sorts of goodies. After dinner, we would play beauty parlor. We would cut Grandpa's fingernails and toenails. We would also cut his nose and ear hairs. When we were done, we would get ready for The Gong Show. That was our favorite show. When it was over, we would get cuddled into Grandpa's bed. He would sing us a song that started, "See-saw knock at the door, who's there? Grandpa. What do you want? A glass of beer. Where's your money? In my pocket. Where's your pocket? In my pants. Where's your pants? In the closet. Get out of here, you stinking bum." That's how I remember it anyway.

Back at home, we had these lovely old folks, Mr. and Mrs. Wilson, who lived next door to us. The wife gave my sister and me these beautiful gowns to play with. I felt like I was Cinderella, wondering if my prince would ever come. They always gave us candy and things. We didn't know them long before we moved in. One night—and this is a little creepy— I thought I was having a dream. I was thinking of Mrs. Wilson next door, and I saw her reach for something high up in the cabinet and then fall to the floor. About an hour or so later, I heard sirens, and I looked out the window to see the police next door. I hopped back into bed. When I awoke the next morning, I just thought I had had a bad dream. When I saw "Mother" in the kitchen, she told me and my sister that Mrs. Wilson had passed away during the night. I just sat there, dumbfounded; everything drained out of me. All the good people leave my life. So it wasn't a dream after all. I felt like it was my fault.

I never told anyone about Mrs. Wilson until about seventeen years later, when I told my aunt, who was my mother's sister and my godmother. "Mother" told me that she and her sister hadn't spoken to their two brothers in fifteen years. I'm not sure what the argument was about. I believe it was over my grandfather. Some years later, they started talking to each another, but it was never the same. We had been a close-knit family, and now we were kind of distant. I had a great relationship with my aunt and uncle; they were also my godparents. Every other weekend, my aunt and uncle would take me for the weekend. My uncle would pick me up and bring me to their house, where my aunt would be waiting. Then we would get ready to go out to dinner. After dinner, we would always go to Times Square Stores, and they would buy me a new Barbie doll. I was so close to them that I was able to tell them what was going on at home. I was also close to their children, my cousins. Sometimes they would pick me up and take me out.

Eventually "Mother" put a stop to me going there. Sometimes my aunt got in the middle, but nothing ever came of it. Little did my parents know that every

Friday night, when they went food shopping, I would call my aunt and talk to her about what was still going on at home. When I was six years old, I was an angry little girl. I would cut the hair off my Barbie dolls and then take their clothes off and put them against each another. Back then I didn't know why I did what I did. Later on, you'll understand why I did half the stuff I did. It wasn't done on purpose. I'm not saying I was perfect, because I was nowhere near perfect. We all have flaws.

Our family wasn't a happy family. Our family was always in some type of turmoil. My father was having problems with drinking, and "Mother" had some issues. She was always complaining about pains in her chest or crying. I thought there was something wrong with her. "Mother" and my dad fought all of the time. Sometimes when Dad got home from work, you knew he had been drinking. "Mother" would start in on him, and the kitchen table would go flying with the food on it, or "Mother" would throw meat on the floor. I have to say, my dad did work hard as a mechanic and also a taxi driver for a while, but "Mother" would spend money she didn't have. She was always impulsive, and Dad would get angry. Sometimes Dad put holes in the walls because he got so angry.

I felt that because "Mother" was so unhappy, she took it out on me. I was the black sheep in the family. "Mother" never had an excuse to beat the crap out of me, but she did it anyway. When she would hit me, I would crawl to the floor because I was so frightened. She would say things like "I could kill you" with such viciousness in her eyes. Not only was the abuse physical, but it was also verbal. My mother and father would say things like, "You're stupid, a lost cause to society, and a moron." The bruises and broken bones can heal, but words stay with you forever. It was like a seed was embedded in me, and I believed everything they said. Whatever self-esteem I had went down the drain. Anybody can have broken bones, but when people keep calling you the same bad names over and over again, of course you're going to believe you're stupid, you're no good. I talk about the beatings I have gotten from both parents, but the name-calling really stayed with me. I eventually believed everything I had been told. To me, "Mother" was telling me I should have never been born. This is the trick with verbal abuse: unless you get help and are around more positive people, you will continue to think you're this horrible person. But the positive people reinforce what you really are. Eventually, you hear it enough, and you begin to believe. Today

I know I am a good mom, I am a good person, and I have a big heart with a lot to give. The one big outcome of all this is that I finally like myself.

I don't remember how old I was, but one day my sister and I were playing outside. I saw a yellow jacket on the ground and picked it up. I thought it was dead, and I was teasing her with it. I hated her as much as "Mother." "Mother" heard her screaming. She took my hand, opened it, put the yellow jacket in it, closed my fist, and it stung me. What kind of a mother does that to her child? She could have punished me, but this was a dreadful way to do it.

I remember one other time. It was almost Christmas, and my sister and I were coloring. I remember my sister asking if Santa Claus was real. She was five years old, and I was seven. I told her that he wasn't real. She started crying, and my parents came into the living room to find out what was wrong. My sister told my parents what I told her, and I got punished. I don't remember what kind of punishment it was.

I started first grade at Gotham Avenue School, which was three blocks from our house. School was a rough time for me. I was having difficulty academically, and I was left behind to repeat second grade. The next second-grade teacher really helped me to succeed, but I still struggled. Kids were bullying me all the time. "Mother" was too into her shit to see that I needed help. In elementary school I was in a play called The Wizard of Oz. I played one of the munchkins. I liked the boy who played the Tin Man; his name was Dave. He said, he asked me out years later. I said yes, but when he came to my house to pick me up, I didn't go with him. I don't remember why. I also liked this other kid, and I remember some kids found out and picked us both up by our legs and arms. They pushed us on top of each other, and I scraped my arms and legs. My fifth grade teacher was the worst. All she would do is yell at me for no reason. I don't remember why she did or if I told anyone. She reminded me of "mothe'r. These are the only memories I have of elementary school.

Then, one day, I remember my aunt coming to pick up my sister and me early from school. She was my "mother's" brother's wife. I kept asking her why? When we got to her house, I saw an ambulance and police cars at my grandfather's house. My aunt sat us down and told us that Grandpa went to heaven. I was about twelve, and that was my first wake. All I remember is standing outside. I don't even know if I went in. That's the last thing I remember about that.

The only good thing actually about Gotham Avenue School was our gym teacher, Mr. Franklin. He was a great guy and was always there for you. I also remember graduation day in the auditorium. I was so happy that I was moving on to middle school. I was hoping that it was going to be a better experience for me.

CHAPTER 2

MIDDLE SCHOOL

I remember my father's mother and father, my grandparent's. She was cold. When you went to kiss her, she would give you her cheek. My grandfather, on the other hand, was the nicest man. One time they took my sister and me to Atlantic City for the weekend. That's the only good time I remember. We would see them maybe every two weeks. I was still having issues at home, and I remember a place called Sunrise something in Hempstead, New York. It was a place where they helped children and their families. One day I was driving down Hempstead Turnpike, and I saw a street named Wolcott, which caught my eye. That's when the memory came back to me. I was put into temporary foster care. I remember staying with this family. They were so nice. I asked them if I could live with them, but they told me I would have to go back home. That's not what I wanted to hear.

Eventually, I came back home and entered middle school, which was a part of the high school. I figured that since my cousins were in the school, they would be there to protect me. But they really didn't do much. People just walked into you and didn't say a word. Again, I was having trouble academically. But I had such wonderful teachers. They tried hard to help me. My reading teacher, Mrs. Stone, was great, and she helped me to finally pass reading. There was one other teacher, my resource room teacher. It was a class for children with learning disabilities. She helped me with all my classes. We stayed in touch for a while and then lost contact.

"Mother" would send me to school all dressed up and with my hair done. I hated it. Everyone was always making fun of me. They were all dressed in jeans and sneakers. So I asked "Mother" If I could wear jeans just like everyone else. She said I could only on the two gym days. She just didn't want to understand what I was going through. Nothing changed; I was constantly bullied, and pushed, and shoved around like an animal.

People don't to think about maybe that person is having a bad day. Or maybe going there going through something. They rather be mean and obnoxious. Then One day, after leaving school a little late, I was walking around the corner when five guys from school grabbed me and shoved me into a bunch of bushes. They started poking me with sticks and touching me all over. I kept screaming and trying to get away. Luckily, my cousin happened to be looking for me, because I was so late. He saw what they were doing to me and told me to run home. I told "Mother" what happened, and she never said a word. "Mother" had called all of these boys fathers whom she went to school with earlier in her life. They all came to my house with their sons.

I thought I was humiliated then, but this was worse: every guy had to apologize to me and leave me alone. I was so afraid to go back to school the next day, but things were quiet. Don't get me wrong; I was still bullied. Back then no one understood anything about bullying. Too many children and teens committed suicide due to being bullied. Thank God that today there is more awareness about how many children are being bullied, and plenty of things are being done about it.

The only close friend that I had at the time lived around the corner from me. We did everything together. We rode our bikes almost every day for hours. Some days we just played board games. I would eat at her house and sleep over. Her parents were the sweetest. One day, while riding our bikes, we met these guys who were a little older than us, and we started hanging out with them after school. I was attracted to one guy, Robert. We would go see them every other day. I guess I was about fifteen or sixteen by then. Robert had asked me to go out, and I got up the nerve and asked "Mother" if I could go out with him. I told her he was picking up his older brother at the train station, and then we were going to see a movie. I was surprised when she said yes.

The evening of our date Robert was almost an hour late. When he showed up at the door, "Mother" said I couldn't go. I begged her to let me go. "Mother" said no, but Dad said to go and to be home by midnight. I honestly thought we were going to see a movie, and Robert said he had to stop at his friend's house. I was scared, but I went. Robert told me to look in the newspaper to see what movies were playing, so I guessed I was going to have to lie to my parents. I asked why, and he said he had a surprise for me. What did I know? It was my first time going on a date. We stopped at some warehouse, which was scary. He went in, and ten minutes later he came out. He wouldn't tell me why he went in there, just that it was business. Then we were driving, and I kept asking where we were going, and Robert finally said we were going to Lover's Lane. I didn't know what Lover's Lane was. Now, mind you, we had his brother's car. I saw a bridge and a few cars around. What little I could see was people making out. I didn't want to be a baby and tell him to take me home, so we started making out, and we felt the car settling down. Robert got out of the car; we had gone too far out in the marsh, and the car was sinking.

We tried so hard to get it out, but we couldn't. Robert called his brother and told him what happened. We had to call for a tow truck. Now it was way past my curfew. What was I going to tell my parents? I called them on the pay phone, and I don't remember what I said or if it was the truth or not, but they were pissed. Back then there were no cell phones. We had to wait for a tow truck, and then I was taken home. When I finally got home, it was around two o'clock in the morning. My father was standing at the front door and yelling at Robert. He told Robert to forget my name, my address, and my number. I was so embarrassed. I got whipped with the belt and sent to bed. I saw Robert only once or twice more, and after that, my relationship with my best friend was over. Then she became friends with my sister. I was so hurt. I lost the only friend I had. I had made one mistake.

I did have another friend from school, that I somewhat was close with. Sometimes when things weren't going so well at home; I would spend the weekend at her house. We had fun playing games and just making girl talk. We were friends for quite some time but I don't remember what happened, but we didn't see much of each other anymore.

When I was sixteen, I started dating this guy, Frank, who was a senior in my school. I remember always hanging out at his friend's house. We rarely went anywhere except to his house once in a while. One day, while hanging out, we were making out, and he asked me to have sex with him. I was scared; it would be my first time. What was I going to say? No? Then he'd never want to be with me. So we had sex, and I felt so disgusting after that. It didn't even do anything for me. Then it continued a few times more. He wanted me to take a shower with him, but that's where I drew the line. He had asked me to his prom; I bought a dress, and his dad was a seamstress and fixed it for me. His parents were a very nice, quiet Italian couple. We went in a limousine with a few of his friends. I had the worst time. We mostly sat at the table, and I really didn't know anyone. When it was time for me to go home, I was dropped off. I wasn't allowed to go with Frank and his friends to the beach the next day. Frank and I would write sexy notes back and forth to each other. I had them in my desk, and "Mother" found them and was fuming. I asked Frank to take me to my aunt's house. "Mother" knew I was there and came later. She sat in a chair across from me and asked why I had sex with Frank. All I could say was that I didn't know why. I really didn't.

I'm still sixteen years old. "Mother," my cousin, my sister, and I were sitting at the table, playing cards. "Mother" and my cousin were smoking. "Mother" asked me if I wanted to try one. I felt like one of the adults. I put it in my mouth and I choked; it was disgusting. When I would hang out with my cousin, she would teach me how to smoke. I did get used to it, but I had no money and was too young to buy my own cigarettes. "Mother" never knew my sister was smoking. "Mother" would leave several packs of cigarettes out every day. So every morning, before school, my sister took a few cigarettes with her to school. I followed what she did. One day, when my sister had already left for school, I grabbed a cigarette, put it in a tissue, and put it at the bottom of my pocketbook. Right after "Mother" had woke up, she came downstairs and went straight to my pocketbook. She emptied everything out, unwrapped the tissue, and found the cigarette. She beat me and told me to never touch another cigarette. I walked out the door, crying, to school. I walked into the nurse's office, and she asked me if I wanted to press charges against "Mother." I was so afraid of her that I said no. I constantly ran away from home and stayed with different friends, and then I would have to go back home.

One day, I decided to try out to become a cheer-leader. I was surprised when I got the call that they had accepted me. I began practicing every day after school. One day, I saw this guy looking at me. The next day, I saw him in school, and he introduced him-self as Anthony. He was so cute. We started seeing each other at his house and at school. He eventually asked me to be his girlfriend. Anthony wore a glove on his right hand, and I asked him why he wore it. He told me that one Fourth of July, someone threw an M80 in his window; when he picked it up to throw it out the window, it blew up in his hand and took off a couple of his fingers. But he was the nicest guy, and we dated for quite some time. One night, he came to a basketball game where I was going to cheer. At half-time, we took a walk outside and made out. I didn't know then that my parents were there, sitting in the car and watching me. You know how I found out? I had a hickey on my neck, but "Mother" waited until after it was gone to tell me that they had been there. I got the third degree. They were like vultures, just waiting for me to do something wrong.

One day at school, a couple of kids were show-ing one another their birth certificates. I looked at them; I had never had one. I went home and asked "Mother" if I could have my birth certificate. The following, she handed me a big copy of it with my name, my parents' names, and my date of birth. It looked nothing like the other kids' certificates. I called my aunt and told her how I felt, and she told me it wasn't her responsibility. I knew something was wrong. In a way, I think she wanted me to know, and I asked her what she meant. She told me to ask "Mother." I was at a friend's house at the time, so I left and went home. I explained to "Mother" that other students showed me their birth certificates, and I told her mine didn't look right. She went into her pocketbook and said she was going to show me hers, but it wasn't there. She told me that she was married to my father, got divorced, and then married this man who I called Father. She told me she got married, and years later he adopted my sister and me. "Mother" told me that she told my father that I knew, and he was very upset. "Mother" said that when he came home, I should tell him that I love him. She couldn't tell someone how to feel about someone else, but I did tell him I loved him because I was afraid of her. The next day, I called my aunt and asked her for information about my biological father. We met for coffee. She told me that I looked just like my father; I had his round nose. She told me that their marriage didn't work out and that he just left me and never looked back. He also never paid any child support. I had to soak all of this in. I also found out that my sister was my half-sister; "Mother" had her out of wedlock with a man she supposedly loved. So why did she have to make a big deal out of it when it happened to me? You'd think she would have been more supportive and understanding. Why did she have to treat me so badly? She wasn't so innocent.

I had such hatred toward "Mother" that I had a plan. One day, while I was sitting on the stoop, I thought of how I could kill "Mother." She stood on a ladder, cutting her forsythia bushes. I was thinking in my head about how could I kill her and make it look like an accident. I thought of walking by and kicking the ladder. She would fall down, and the shears would go into her chest. I didn't do it, but I wanted revenge; instead, life went on as usual.

I got a job at Times Square Stores. I befriended a much older girl. After a few months, she asked me if I would like to go to her boyfriend's promotion party. I asked my parents, and they said yes. I had a curfew at midnight. My friend picked me up, and we went to the party. When we got there, people were acting weird. Someone came over to me and asked if I would like a drink. I had a little wine, and I started feeling really weird. I was dizzy and wanted to throw up. I was holding the walls and asked where the bathroom was.

When I got to the bathroom, the bowl felt like it kept moving. I was hugging the bowl. I must have been there for thirty minutes. Then someone took me over to a couch, and I guess I passed out. When I got up, I still wasn't feeling well, and I told my girlfriend that I wanted to go home. She put me in a car with some guys, who were supposed to be going home. I was still throwing up and must have blacked out, because I don't know what happened. I was in the backseat, and I believe all of those guys took advantage of me. I don't know how long it was before we returned to my friend's house. I did not know why or what had just happened, but I believe I was drugged and possibly raped. I was passed out in the backseat. I knew I couldn't go home, because I knew they would never believe me, so I stayed with my friend. I know I was wrong for not going home, but knowing what I would come home to made me scared. I couldn't take another beating. There was no talking to my parents. I ended up living with my friend, and I didn't talk to my parents for several months. I went to work during the day and would go out at night. One night, her car got stuck in the middle of the road. A car pulled up behind us full of auxiliary police, and they were friends of hers. They helped get the car to their building.

One guy was named John, and the other was Jimmy. I was attracted to Jimmy, but I was being pushed toward John. Jimmy took me with him to get a tire for the car. When we got back, John kept pushing himself on me. Jimmy and I had made plans to see one another.

The following day, I thought it was Jimmy who called to make plans to pick me up. When it was time, I saw a car pull up, but when I opened the door it was John. I asked where Jimmy was. He said he was going to take me to him. I was hesitant about getting in a car with someone I hardly knew. We ended up at some bar. I asked again where Jimmy was, and he said Jimmy wasn't meeting me; it was John who had called me. We got a drink and talked.

I really wasn't sure what to do. I just always wanted someone to love and care for me. I found all the wrong men. I never understood why I did this. I didn't like it, but I didn't know how to get out of it. It was almost five o'clock in the morning, and we drove into a parking lot.

John asked me if I ever saw the sunrise. After the sun rose, we drove into a driveway. I asked where we were, and he said he didn't know. A few minutes later, he laughed and said it was his house. We went in, went to his room, and went to sleep. When we got up the next morning, he introduced me to his aunt and uncle. I found out that John owned a limousine service with his aunt. She took the calls, and he drove people all over. I didn't know what I was supposed to do with myself. I didn't even know where he lived. I took a walk one day and realized we were in Queens somewhere. I decided to go to a temp agency to get a job. I remember taking a typing test and a computer test. I was supposed to go back, but John wanted me to stay at the house. John told me I wasn't allowed to leave the house. One day, while John was at work, I called Jimmy. He picked me up, and we had a really nice time. He was teaching me how to drive. When I got home, John was waiting for me. He was pissed and told me I couldn't see Jimmy. John was a crazy person. He wanted to have sex and I didn't. He ripped my clothes off and pushed himself inside me on the couch. Then he took out his handcuffs from being an auxiliary police officer, and he handcuffed me to a door in the living room and made me stay there all night. This went on for months. I couldn't take the abuse anymore and decided to call my parents. I think I explained part of what happened, but not all of it. They didn't need to know the details. I returned back home.

I was still sixteen, and I don't know what happened with school since I was away for a while. But I do remember another incident that happened with a friend from school. My friend's cousin had graduated from high school, and his parents were having a party. My cousin asked me if I wanted to go and to sleep over at her house afterward. I asked my parents if I could go, and they said yes. We went to the party, and her cousin became interested in me. I was supposed to go home with my friend's mother, but my friend asked her mother if we could stay. I figured that my parents couldn't find out. My friend's cousin asked his parents if he could drive us home; he had just received his license. His parents told him to take us straight there and back. We had to stop at Friendly's. I sat in the car. Then they got in the car and dropped off my friend's brother at her house. I was wondering why we weren't getting out. We drove around the corner and everyone was talking and then her cousin started making out with me. I said, "That's enough. We have to go back." Then he said his cousin and her guy just started making out, so we had to wait until they were done. All of a sudden, bright lights shined behind us. My friend's cousin's father started screaming at him and told him to go back home. We got dropped off at my friend's house, and her mother told me to call my parents. My girlfriend's mom had to call my parents to see if we were there. Why in the world would we be there? I got dropped off at home, and there was dad, giving me the third degree and the belt. I got the belt and was sent to bed. I honestly did not want to go with them, but they would think I was a baby. Today I don't care what people think of me. They either like me, or they don't.

CHAPTER 3

EIGHTEEN

The next chapter of my life starts at eighteen years old. I had finally finished high school. I had finally made it to that special day and was getting out of there! I was able to graduate on my normal graduation date, because I had all my credits. We were having graduation rehearsal when Mrs. Bradley pulled me over and told me I wasn't graduating. I didn't understand what was going on, so I left. I went home and told my "Mother," but she made no attempt to call the school to find out what happened. I was so down that I went to stay with my aunt and uncle. On Sunday, "Mother" called me to tell me they were looking for me on graduation day. Somebody screwed up, and I missed the best day of my life.

A friend I met at school asked me if I wanted to go out on a double date. I was going on a blind date with her boyfriend's friend. I was stunned when I saw him, because he was not good-looking at all, but I went with it. We went to some kind of club and had several drinks. I looked for my friend, because I wanted to go home, but she was nowhere in sight. Whoever this guy was, I asked him to stop and take me home.

We ended up in an alley, and he wanted to kiss me. I asked him to stop and to please take me home. I got lucky this time, and he took me home. I don't really remember if I saw my friend after that. That's the only memory I have of it. However, the next memory is about another time I left home; I don't remember why, but I left home again and lived in Malverne, New York. I was watching children to earn free room and board. When I was walking with the kids one day, I spotted this school. It was called European American Beauty School. I walked inside and asked if they had financial aid. They said yes, so I applied to the school. I decided to go at night. It was actually a lot of fun, and I passed my tests.

I still have more stories about the men in my life. I met Joe when I was eighteen years old, when I was invited to a friend's party, and he was the bartender. He took a break, and we sat and talked for a while. We hit it off. We had so much in common. We started dating. We would go to antique shows, ride our bikes, and go out dancing a lot. It was the 1980s, and it was a great time. I was having the time of my life, the best fun I had had in a long time. One day, his sister was driving us to the beach. Joe's sister was making a left-hand turn. I never saw it, but Joe said it was too late to say anything. A car T-boned us, and I got hurt. We went to the hospital to get checked out, but we only had some cuts and bruises. Joe and I had to walk from Long Beach all the way back to Malverne. That was the longest walk I had ever taken. We had been dating more than three years, and I thought he was the love of my life.

I had lost my babysitting job and had nowhere to go. I stayed at Joe's house for two days. I then went to my priest and explained my situation. He told me about this woman who took people in from time to time. So Joe took me there to meet her. She seemed nice; she worked all day, had a son who lived upstairs and a daughter who lived downstairs, and she had a son who was married and in the reserves. Everything was going great. One day, we took a ride to the airport to pick up her son, who was in the reserves, and his wife. They seemed to be a nice couple. They surprised me with a birthday cake when I turned nineteen. I thought that was really sweet. I started working for a camp across the street in Elmont. I worked there for a few weeks. One day, the phone rang, and it was the reserves guy. The older son of the women I was living with. He was telling me how beautiful I was and that he wanted me to be one of his prostitutes. He said he would buy me all these beautiful clothes. I told him I was doing nothing like that and hung up the phone. The phone rang again. I picked it up, and he said if I hung up again he would have me thrown out. The next thing I heard was a key going into the door. I was sitting on the couch and saw him walk in. He came over to me and got on top of me. I squeezed my nails in his arms, and he threw me off the couch. I felt so disgusted. I don't know what he said to his mother, but when she got home, she told me to pack my bags and get out. I tried to explain to her, but she didn't want to hear anything. I called Joe, and he came to pick me up.

I was very close to the lady who taught the class at the school. I told her in a nutshell what happened, and she had a solution for me. We made an agreement that I would watch her kids, and then when she came home I would go to school at night. Things were working out. The only thing a little strange about her was that she had a voodoo room. She showed it to me once and said I could never go in there. That was fine by me. Then I had another altercation. I heard someone coming in the front door, and he introduced himself as her ex-husband. She never told me he would stop by. He just came in, introduced himself, and then went upstairs. I went back to the kids. About thirty minutes later, I heard him calling me. He was standing in a towel at the top of the stairs. He took his finger and pointed for me to come over to him. I said no and went back to playing with the kids. I called Joe and told him what happened. I asked him what I should do. He told me to tell the woman I was staying with. When she came home, I asked her to sit down, and I told her that I had something important to tell her. I told her, and she grabbed me by my hair and started beating the crap out of me. I ran out of the house, and she pulled me back in the house by my hair. Then she took my hand and dug her teeth into the palm of it. It hurt like a son of a bitch. She was a lunatic. Her ex came back, and I asked him to intercede. He still denied what he had done. I don't know how long it was, but it felt like forever when Joe pulled up. She put all my clothes into black garbage bags.

When Joe saw what I looked like, he was screaming at her. But before I left, she whispered in my ear, "If you ever tell anyone what happened here, I will have you splattered all over the ground." She really scared me. I believed her after all of that. Joe took me to my friend's house for the night. I have to tell you, she was also into voodoo. What a night I was having. She said she was going to put a spell on her, but I didn't believe in that shit. I went to get some clothes out of the bags when I realized she put dog shit in them. My friend asked me to take a ride back to the woman's house; she wanted to show me something. I know you won't believe this, because I myself was in shock at the time. We went back to that woman's house in West Babylon, and her voodoo room was on fire, and there were fire trucks there. I never said another word. She said, "See, that's the spell I put on her."

I was afraid to go back to school with the woman there. I waited a few days until she was off, and then I went inside to talk to the owners. They could not believe how bad I looked. I had bruises all over and teeth marks in the palm of my right hand. They told me not to be afraid; they would keep an I on her.

They wanted me to finish. With all that, I didn't have the self-confidence to take the state test. I went through all of that for nothing. The owners of my school decided to take me in. They were European and very nice people. They had two older sons in their thirties, and they were adopting a fifteen-year-old. She was always getting into trouble. She had a friend named Danny. We became close friends. He was really nice, too, but for some reason I never kept in touch with the good people. I guess it's because I was always on the run somewhere. I started working for one of the owners' sons, who had his own hair salon. He would let me do manicures and pedicures for money, and I would also cut the men's hair. I was good at that; women's hair was harder for me. He let me do that with no license. He was taking a risk, which I really appreciated.

Joe was the love of my life. He went through so much with me. I didn't blame him when I found out he was cheating on me. Why would he want someone who was always getting into some kind of trouble? But of course my heart was broken. After a few months, I wound up going back home again. I guess I was happier if I got some kind of attention, even if it was negative. I got very sick over the breakup with Joe. I became anorexic, and I was throwing up every day. I was being self-destructive. I wound up weighing eighty pounds.

One day, when I was waiting for the bus, Joe passed by on his way to work. He saw me and asked me what happened. I told him that I loved him, and I was heartbroken. That was the last time I saw him.

Whenever I asked to come home, it wasn't "Mother" who said yes. It was always my dad. Sometimes I felt like it was out of guilt because he adopted me and he felt that obligation. So they let me come home, and I had a lot of explaining to do again. Months later, as I was walking home from church, I was coming back through my school parking lot when a black man grabbed me from behind and pushed me to the ground. I don't know where I got my strength from, but I pushed him off and started screaming, running all the way home. I wasn't thinking that he had followed me all the way to my house. Now he knew where I lived. I told "Mother." We called the police. They came to the house, took me to the police station, and asked me if I could pick him out of the mug-shot books.

The photographs all looked the same, and I really didn't get a good look at him. I was so scared! My sister's husband told me to take a can of hair spray with me to work, so I could spray it at him and run. When I got off the bus at the end of the day, I was walking past the second block when I saw him waiting at the corner of my block. I started screaming, and my sister came running out! We called the police. They came and looked around, but they couldn't find him. But I was thankful, because after that I never saw him again.

I decided it was time for me to get my driver's license. I couldn't stand taking the bus anymore. I failed my first test because I had no self-confidence. I tried a second time and passed. I saved up about $2,000 from my job to get a car. Since my dad was a mechanic, I asked him if he could help me get a car. He told me a friend of his had one for $3,500. It was a Pontiac. My parents told me my grandfather had left me some money when he died, so they could add that to my $2,000. But when my sister went to Barbizon School, they used the money for her to go there and to buy all of her clothes, and it wasn't cheap. My grandfather left us both more than $2,000 each. I wanted to know what happened to the rest of mine. I never asked, because I knew what the answer would be. I was hurt and angry that they couldn't give me my fair share. But there was nothing I could do about it. After all that, my sister never did anything with her modeling career. That was a waste of money.

CHAPTER 4
AUNT AND UNCLE

B y now, my aunt and uncle had retired and moved from Farmingdale to New Jersey. I hadn't seen them in a long time, so I decided to surprise them and spend the weekend with them. I had made it almost all the way down the New Jersey Turnpike when I heard a loud noise. I pulled over and saw that my muffler was hanging on the ground. I called my aunt and told her. They had it towed to a place that could have it ready by Sunday to get home. It was so good to see them. We sat and talked for a while, and as usual we went out to dinner and walked around the mall. We spent the weekend around the house. It was just so nice to be with them again.

My cousin and her husband showed up unexpectedly on Saturday, which sucked. They just decided to take a ride out on the same weekend I was going. On Sunday, I was ready to pick up my car. My aunt told my cousin to let me follow them home. Well, they made one stop. After that, I completely lost them. I tried my best to get home. I kept going through tolls and paying money, not knowing where I was. Finally, I saw a tollbooth worker and explained to him that I wanted to get to Long Island. He said I was in Manhattan. He stopped traffic, let me turn around, and told me how to get home. It took me almost four hours.

A few weeks after I saw my aunt and uncle, my parents went to spend the weekend with them. They were playing cards, and a card fell, and my uncle reached down to get it. A couple of days later, "Mother" got a call from my aunt; she said that my uncle wasn't feeling good and that he was very cold. My aunt called for an ambulance, and when they got to the front of the hospital, my uncle had a heart attack, and they had to resuscitate him. They brought him back, but he was never the same again. They said that the night they were playing cards, a piece of bone chipped off inside my uncle's body and went straight to his heart. "Mother" stayed with her sister for months until my uncle was able to come home. When he came to visit, I saw this frail man in a wheelchair, not a man who used to be six foot two and have a decent build. Everything drained from my body. What I saw was not my uncle. I loved him like a father. He looked at me. I kissed him and told him I loved him very much.

I was now working for a mortgage company. While I was at work, I got a phone call that my uncle had passed away. I felt weak and passed out. My boss told me to go home.

When they had the wake, it was hard for me to even walk. My legs started to collapse, and my cousin's husband grabbed me and helped me walk to the casket. I gave him my last kiss good-bye, and he was so cold. They had a veteran's ceremony because he had been in the service. It was so hard to hear the guns go off. Chills went through my body. I couldn't believe he was gone.

CHAPTER 5

HAVE FIRST CHILD

I decided that I was twenty-two years old, and it was time for me to move out on my own. I rented an apartment with two other girls. They were all right. My girlfriend from work asked me to go to happy hour at the Marriott. When we got there, all these handsome guys were in suits. My girlfriend and I were sitting at the bar when the bartender came over and handed us each a drink. We asked who had ordered them, and she pointed to a guy who sat across from us. I didn't know what to do, so my girlfriend asked him to come over. We started having a conversation, and my friend disappeared. Jeff and I danced for hours. I tried looking for my friend to take me home, but she was nowhere in sight. Jeff offered to take me home.

I didn't want to go with someone I didn't know, but he seemed like an honest guy. Jeff was divorced and a vice principal of an elementary school. Things were going pretty well. We went to clubs on the weekends. I noticed that every time he drank, he got nasty. He would only drink on the weekends. He took me to meet his mom, who lived upstate. She was a very nice lady, but she said, "What are you doing with an alcoholic?" I was shocked and said nothing. I didn't know he was an alcoholic. He came upstate to sign his divorce papers. Then we went to meet his best friends for dinner. It was really nice, and they were very nice people. Then they asked us over to their house. As we were driving to their house, he kept yelling at me to give him a blowjob. Everyone seemed to have control over me. I allowed it for some reason.

Jeff had a lot to drink. I was a little nervous driving home, and I had every right to be. Upstate it is very dark, and all the roads are winding. Jeff started yelling about how much he loved me and that we were going to crash into a tree and be together forever. My heart was in my hands. One night, we went to a club, and I had one drink. He had already had three drinks in the first ten minutes we were there. I told him I felt really sick and needed to leave. He was hyperventilating. After we left, he tore my dress off because I refused to have sex. He forced himself on me.

I couldn't wait until he was done. I was so sick after. That weekend, I was reading in the newspaper that there were different types of alcoholics. One of them was a weekend one. Right away, I realized that's what Jeff was. I tried talking to him, but he came at me, and I grabbed a knife.

He asked, "What do you think you're doing with that?" He grabbed it from me and put it against my throat. He then took it away. I got my things and walked out the door. I went back to my apartment and tried to make myself something to eat. I turned on the oven, and it wasn't getting hot. I saw a hole and forgot what the girls had told me. I took a match and lit it; all of a sudden, a big flame came at me. I tried to turn away from it, but it singed my hair and burned my face and neck. I screamed for my landlady downstairs. She called an ambulance. The doctor told me I was lucky, because I only had second-degree burns, and they gave me special medicine. After months, it all went away, and my hair grew back.

While I was still working at the mortgage company, I decided to go to school at night. I signed up at Nassau Community College. There, I met the most gorgeous guy. Frank had these beautiful, long eyelashes. I was so attracted to him. After a few weeks, we started talking to each other. We would sit in his car and talk for hours. I asked him where he lived, and he told me he lived in an apartment in Garden City, New York. I asked why we never went anywhere. He said he belonged to a gang. He had a girl he was trying to break it off with. He really scared me. I was so naive that it didn't bother me. On school nights, we just sat in his car talking and making out. I also signed up for classes at the Institute of Children's Literature through a magazine. I wanted to learn how to write for children. I wrote a little piece and got a certificate at the end of the class. It was a passion of mine.

Eventually, Frank came over, and we had sex for the first time. He said he could easily fall in love with me. I think those were every guy's famous words to get you into bed. After two months, I wasn't feeling well, and I was gaining some weight. I decided to be tested to see if I was pregnant. The next day, I got the dreaded news that it was positive. I was going to be a mom. I drove around Garden City with my girlfriend to find the apartment building Frank lived in. After about an hour, I finally found it. I left a balloon by the mailbox and a note asking him to marry me. I wanted to call Frank, but I didn't know what his reaction would be. I then got the nerve and called him. I asked him if he could meet me at the school after work. When five o'clock came, I was nervously waiting for him. I saw him pull up next to my car, and he came and sat in the passenger seat. I told him he was going to be a daddy. At first, he was really good about it. He put his arms around me and said it would be ok. Then, he asked me what I was going to do about work and school, said that I was going to lose everything. I told him I didn't know what I was going to do yet. I still had to tell my parents. I called my cousin's wife, who I was close with, and explained everything to her. She told me that until I figured out what I wanted to do, I should just tell them the test was inconclusive. So that's exactly what I did. "Mother" told me I was lying, because she called the doctor, and he told her I was pregnant. I didn't realize she wouldn't have been able to get any information from the doctor. I was twenty-two years old. I was so stupid. She fooled me again. My stepdad and "Mother" were screaming at me. How was I going to bring up a baby? "Mother" said I needed to get an abortion. So she took me to two abortion clinics, and when I saw the rooms, I felt like they were going to chop me up. It was so gloomy. There was just a table and some surgical tools. I ran out of there. She couldn't force me to have an abortion!

I wound up quitting my job. I was working off the books at a friend's gas station in the deli department.

"Mother" asked me for my boss's wife's number. She spoke to his wife, who was very religious, and she told "Mother" about Maria Regina Residence. It was run by nuns, and they took care of girls who were pregnant up until their babies were born. "Mother" and I both spoke to the psychologist there separately. I kept thinking, where was I going to go with a baby and no money? I was so upset that I had to give up my car. All the girls had their own chores to do. Sometimes we would go on trips. I hated it so much. I called every day and asked "Mother" if I could come back home, but she kept refusing. She didn't want any neighbors to know I was having a baby.

My aunt told me to pray to the dead. Someone you were close with will answer your prayers. One day, while praying to my uncle, I was looking up at the ceiling and I saw my uncle. I know this sounds a little crazy, but I saw him smiling at me with his hands reaching down to me. It was like he was telling me everything was going to be all right. I called "Mother" again and told her I could get food stamps and pay her rent. She finally said yes. I was due in two months. When I told the psychologist, she told me it wasn't a good idea, especially with a baby. The psychologist could tell what "Mother" was like by talking with her. But I had nowhere to go. I was finally home and "Mother" put me downstairs, which was just a musty brick basement. My bed, a dresser, and the baby's crib were there.

About a month later, I woke up with these terrible cramps. I realized I was in labor. I had to crawl up ten steps to the kitchen, then crawl to the living room and yell upstairs to my parents that it was time. I heard "Mother" wake my father and tell him that it was time. We got into the car, and I sat in the backseat. "Mother" couldn't even sit back there with me to comfort me. We got to the hospital, and they wheeled me into a room. I had front and back labor. It was awful. I was in labor for fourteen hours. They brought me to another room to give me an episiotomy. My canal was too small to push her through. Before I knew it, at 1:48 a.m., I had a beautiful, big, brown-eyed baby girl at the age of twenty-three. Kimberly had so much hair. It was the most amazing thing ever. They wheeled us out into the hallway for everyone to see. "Mother," my aunt, and my family were filled with joy. "Mother" was ecstatic for someone who had wanted me to get rid of her.

I don't know what "Mother" or anyone told my cousins, but it seemed like time stood still. All of my cousins stopped talking to me. They all moved out of state. I knew what states they were in, but that's all I knew, and no one would give me any information. I would love to reconnect with them, to find out why they stopped talking to me, and to hopefully maybe have a relationship again. I have no family in my life. I'd love to know why they separated from me, because we used to be so close. I can only assume that life got in the way. I hope one day that we will be able to reconnect. I have also tried to find my aunt. The last time I saw her is when she had a stroke about fifteen years ago. All I know is that she lives in Orlando, Florida, and she is ninety-two years old now. I miss her terribly, and before anything happens I would love to say hello. I have tried finding them, but I guess they are private. I wanted to talk to them and find out what happened. I wanted some unfinished business to be finished. But it doesn't look like that is going to happen. So it's just another part of my life that I have to put behind me. It seems I'm always putting things behind me—too much baggage for such a young person.

When we got home from the hospital, mostly "Mother" took over like my daughter was her child. Kimberly was very colicky. You had to walk around with her to try and help her pass gas. My parents will tell you that I did nothing to help out, but they had decided she was their child, and they were going to do what they wanted to do. Nothing changed at home. "Mother" would yell at me for stupid shit, and I would get stressed out while holding Kimberly, and

Kimberly would get upset. When "Mother" yelled at me while Kimberly was sitting on the floor, she would shake from the screaming. I was so stressed once that I was rocking Kimberly back and forth on my shoulder while sitting on the couch, and I lightly hit her head on the wall. l was afraid to tell them because I knew what they would think, but I wanted to make sure she was all right.

The next day I told "Mother," and from then on I was a horrible mother. My daughter was no longer mine. We had no bond. Kimberly called "Mother" her mama. I called the psychologist at Maria Regina and told her what was happening. She told me I needed to get out of there. I decided it was time for me to get out. I had some friends help me find an apartment. It wasn't much, but it was enough for Kimberly and me. When "Mother" found out, she was pissed. She told me she would hold on to Kimberly until I got the place straightened out.

Again, I wasn't thinking. I should have never trusted her. It took me two weeks, and I went back to "Mother," and she said I was not getting my daughter. I drove to the police station and explained everything to them. The officer called "Mother" and told her she had no right. "Mother" asked me what the officer's name was. I was so overwhelmed that I never got his name. I had to drive all the way back to the police station to get his name. He called "Mother" again. When I finally got Kimberly back, my brother-in-law answered the door and handed me Kimberly with a bottle and diaper. He told me that was all I was getting. I called my friends and told them what had happened. One of them called a church and told them what happened and what I needed. They gave me a crib and toys. Others stocked me up with food. Kimberly was now about eighteen months old. I thought it was time for her father to meet her.

It was Valentine's Day. I called Frank, and he said that he would come. He came, and he saw her for about ten minutes. Then all he wanted was sex. I told him I was going to take him to court for child support. I wouldn't let "Mother" see her for two weeks. Then she called and asked if she could she please see Kimberly. I broke down and let her see her on weekends. One weekend, I went back to pick her up, and "Mother" took me aside and told me she was taking me to court to take Kimberly away from me.

At that time in my life, I was working for a family who owned an advertising agency. They were all so nice. I was upset, and they asked me what was wrong. I told them what "Mother" was going to do. They gave me their lawyer's name to call. I had a nice chat with him, and he told me they had no leg to stand on. I then called "Mother" and told her what my lawyer said. "Mother" got really quiet. She knew she couldn't do anything. It was one of her tactics again.

I eventually took Frank to court. It was great when the judge held up the blood test and said, "This is a home run." What a cool judge he was. But Frank said he didn't have a job and couldn't pay anything. The judge said he had two legs and he could go and find a job. Frank got away with paying fifty dollars a month when he did pay. Every once in a while; he would send in a bigger check. He had to or they would suspend his license for not paying.

CHAPTER 6
BIOLOGICAL FATHER

I felt at this stage in the game that it was time to find my biological father. I wanted to know the other part of me. I would maybe have some family and stability in my life. I had a priest I was close to at my church, and I called him and explained the situation. He said he would look for the baptismal papers and get back to me. Two days later, I heard from the priest. He gave me my father's name. I looked in both the Nassau and Suffolk County phone books to see if he was in them. He was in both, so I wrote to both addresses. A few days later, I received a phone call from a man named Bob. He said he got my letter and that he was my father. He said he had been looking for me for a long time.

I heard people in the background. I discovered I had a half-brother and half-sister. My father was on his third marriage. He asked if he could come meet Kimberly and me. Two nights later, he showed up at the door with a dozen yellow roses for me and a big teddy bear for Kimberly. He showed me some pictures of when I was young. I asked what happened between him and "Mother." He said it didn't work out. Then he married "Mother's" best friend. I told "Mother" and my aunt that I had found my father, and they asked me not to stay in touch with him. But I did, and my aunt didn't talk to me after that. "Mother" was pissed. She said that if she ever saw him, she would stab him with a knife. If they were so adamant about me not seeing him, then why couldn't they explain the reasons to me? I had an idea as to why. "Mother" was the way she was to me because she hated my father so much, and I looked like him. I assume that I reminded her of him, and she took it out on me.

Now my father took us out to dinner, and it was very nice. He told me my grandparents lived two blocks away from me all my life. Isn't that amazing, to know that your flesh and blood were right there? That was so upsetting. I could have known them all my life. My father asked if I wanted to come to his house for the weekend to meet the family.

Everyone was anxious to meet us. I was very curious. He picked us up, and when we pulled up, there were all these people running toward us: my half-sister and half-brother, and Ginger, his second wife, and his best friends. We all went into the backyard and talked for hours. They just adored Kimberly and played with her. My dad had a talk with me. He told me he would help me with my bills. That was a load off my shoulders. I found out he and his wife owned a bowling alley, which was pretty cool. My father asked me if Kimberly and I wanted to move in with them. I was so surprised. I figured I was finally going to have the family I always wanted. I told him I would have to think about it. I was already living in another bad situation. I was living with a girlfriend whose husband had left her for another woman. I had Kimberly, and she had two children who were a little older. We thought we could help each other, so I moved in with her. She gave us one room with a bathroom. But I was able to use the rest of the house. I would share my food stamps and my car with her.

Every weekend, she would go out and bring a different man home and have sex with them. We were in the room next to the living room, so I could hear everything. I didn't want that for my daughter.

After a week, I called my father and asked if I could still live with them. He said yes. That weekend, he came and picked us up. They gave us a room that belonged to his wife's son, and they put him down in the finished basement. Dad said that eventually we could paint our room. Since Dad and his wife were working, I was doing the cleaning and the laundry, and I cooked dinner. That's just the type of person I am. Eventually, Dad told me that they were selling the bowling alley. I had just finished school at Briarcliff College. I was actually graduating from college. I couldn't believe I did it; it was the greatest feeling. My dad bought me a beautiful gold bracelet. In the meantime, I had gotten very close with his second wife. His third wife was a bitch. I spent most of my time with Ginger. When I did spend time with Dad, I was very uncomfortable.

When we finally painted my room, we were all by ourselves. I felt like he was looking right through me, and it made me very uncomfortable. He never helped me with my bills like he told me he would. He told me to get a job. I got a job working at Pathmark and worked there for a while. Then my car broke down. I asked him if he would fix it. He told me to get the part and his friend would fix it. I was just getting screwed all around. Both families were so screwed up. "Mother" never had a picture of me up. She told me I was dead to her. I believe I have always been a good person, but I always got shit on. I realized it was time for Kimberly and me to leave. I just kept putting myself in one frying pan after another.

CHAPTER 7

SECOND CHILD

I found a studio apartment in Bay Shore, New York. I had stopped working and was on welfare, which just paid the rent. I wanted to be home with my daughter.

One day, a friend I met from school came over with her boyfriend. Everyone thought Kimberly was the cutest thing, so they would come over to see her. They had invited me over to her boyfriend's mother's house for Labor Day. That weekend, Kimberly and I went to the Labor Day party. I had the chance to meet my friend's boyfriend's brother. Lee was separated from his wife. He seemed like a nice guy, and his mother was very pleasant. We talked for a while, and he asked me for my number. After a few hours, we went back home. One day, I had to go somewhere, and I asked Ginger if she would babysit for me. I knew she would love to. The next day, I got a call from dad and his third wife, yelling at me. They said that they are the grandparents, and they wanted to know why I didn't ask them. I just told them Ginger asked if she could watch her. I never heard from my dad again. I was fine with it because of the way I felt around my father, and his third wife was a bitch. Lee and I started seeing each other. When we went out, his mom would watch Kimberly. We had been seeing each other for about four months when Lee asked me to marry him. I said yes, and we talked about our plans.

Lee told me that we could get the basement fixed up and live with his mom. I had bought our wedding invitations. I saw him maybe two more times when I found out I was once again pregnant. I was now twenty-six years old. I called Lee to tell him, and he told me he was sick, and he'd call me in a few days. I never heard from him, so I kept trying to call him. I could not believe somebody would do this to me again. I was basically all alone. A month before I was due to have the baby, Lee showed up with pictures from a while ago and a gift basket from his dad for Christmas. He didn't say a word and just turned his back to me and walked out the door.

I was getting really depressed. I heard a message on the radio about a place called Birthright that helps girls who are pregnant. I decided to give them a call. A lady with a very angelic voice answered, and she said her name was Peggy. I explained to Peggy the situation I was in. She made an appointment for me to come and see her. I walked into Birthright with Kimberly and my pregnant belly. Peggy and I talked for a long time. She told me that they help with maternity clothes and baby clothes. Peggy took my number and we kept in touch.

A month later, I called my stepdad and told him I had to go to the hospital. This time the labor was a lot easier. I was in labor for eight hours. First thing after the delivery I called Lee to let him know that he had a son. He told me he would see me later. The nurse asked me what the baby's name was. I had never even thought about it. I was twenty-six years old when I gave birth. I thought about it and realized that Michael Anthony would be his name. He weighed eight pounds, ten ounces. He had such beautiful blue eyes, just like his dad.

Later that evening, I got a call from his father, and he asked if I needed anything. I told him I needed formula and diapers. He showed up with two cans of formula and a package of diapers. What a joke. Like that's going to feed Michael. Then he took him into his arms and put him under the light to see if he looked like him. Then he left. When I got home, I called Lee and told him I was taking him to court. He had to pay child support.

I became friends with another single mom. She had a child the same age as Michael. When she would go shopping, she would steal little things. She showed me how she did it with the baby stroller. I was scared to even try it. Knowing me, I'd be the one to get caught. But one day, we were in Waldies, and I was on welfare and had no money, and I needed clothes for my children. I started stealing, and I would get away with it. It was almost like taking uppers; I was high on stealing! Then one day, we were in the same store, and I had finished and gone out to my car. My friend was taking a long time, so I pulled the car to the front of the door. A police officer approached me and asked me to get out of the car. A lady was taking Michael out of his car seat. The officer put handcuffs on me and brought me back into the store. It was so humiliating to have everyone looking at me. I got caught because my friend told them about me. I gave them the stuff back and told them that my friend had all of her stuff in my trunk. I gave them back everything. The officer said that because I cooperated, they wouldn't press charges. They were going to send me to a shoplifting course. They walked me outside and took off the handcuffs. They handed me a paper telling where and when to go to the shoplifting course.

When I walked into the classroom, I could not believe how many people actually steal. They talked about where the cameras were and that there were security guards dressed just like shoppers who follow customers. They told us that if we ever got caught again, we would be arrested. They also told us we were no longer allowed in that store. That really scared me. I knew I'd never do that again. And I never spoke to that friend again. She wasn't a friend to begin with.

I reached back out to Ginger after I had Michael. I took a ride out to see her. I wanted to introduce her to Michael. Ginger didn't look too good. I asked her what was wrong, and she said she had cancer and didn't have long to live. She was a heavy smoker. I felt awful and so sad for her. She was another good person in my life who I was losing. After we left, I told her I'd come again the following week, but my half-sister called and told me she had already passed away. Another person gone from my life.

We were finally at court when I got the surprise of my life. Lee showed up with a woman and infant. I found out he was back with his wife, and they had a baby around the same age as Michael. We went to have our blood taken to see if he was the father. I knew Michael was his; there was no doubt in my mind.

The following month we had to go back to court to find out the results. The test came back 99.9 percent. My lawyer told me I could ask for what I wanted. I had asked for $275 a week; the number was determined by how much he made. I got that for a couple of months, but then we went back to court because his other son was sick. He couldn't afford the $275 anymore, so they lowered it to $180. That was bullshit. When I talked to my friends from school, they told me they had known about Lee, but they hadn't wanted to tell me and hurt me. Even when Lee asked me to marry him, he was already back together with his wife, and she was pregnant just about the same time as me. After two years, I took Lee back to court and got the original amount I asked for.

Michael's grandmother must have felt some guilt. She was the one who was always taking care of him. She would buy him diapers, clothes, and toys. She was very good to him. One day, Lee's brother and girlfriend and I decided we were going to clean the entire house for her. We found bottles hidden all over her bedroom. She was an alcoholic but never showed it.

Lee sucked at being a father. He saw Michael once a week for about four years. Michael and I had a very special bond. I brought him up all by myself. They never really did anything together but hang out at my place for two hours. One day, Lee brought Michael home from a weekend vacation upstate with his wife. As he was leaving, he told Michael that he didn't want to see him anymore, because he didn't talk to him. Lee needed to grow up. He was so immature. Who says that to his own child? I felt such heartache for my son. I knew how he felt after all I had been through. But it killed me to see my child hurt. Michael never was the same after that; he was depressed and withdrawn.

CHAPTER 8

RAPE

I had joined a mother's group at a church where I could bring Michael and Kimberly. We talked about our children and what was going on in our lives. I met someone named Dotty, and we became pretty good friends. One day, she invited us over for dinner. I asked her if I could do a load of wash, and she said yes. Her husband had invited a friend over as well. After dinner, we stayed for a while. And then we left. When I got home, I put Michael to bed—he was just eight months old, and Kimberly was almost three. I realized that I had left my wash at her house. I called my friend, and she said her husband's friend could drop it off. When he showed up at the door, I suggested he stay for a cup of coffee for bringing over my wash. We talked a little and then we moved onto the couch. The television was already on, because Kimberly had been watching it. But she had fallen asleep on the couch. He then turned my face toward his for a kiss. Then he tried for another one, and I said no. He gave me the line: I could easily fall in love with you. It was a great line to get sex, but I said it was time for him to leave. He got angry and pushed me to the floor. He took one hand and held my two arms above my head, and he used the other hand to pull my pants down. Then he forced himself inside me, and when he was finished, he said thank you and walked out. I just sat there crying for a long time, then got in the shower and cried some more.

I washed the rug. I did not leave the house for days. I didn't want to tell the police, because I knew they would never believe me. They would think I asked for it. My good friend Phil had been calling for days. He got worried and came over, and I opened the door and told him what happened. He told me to call the police; he knew a woman officer. He felt it would be easier for me to talk to her. I told her everything, and then she spoke to a detective. He said he would get back to me. He called me the next day and said the guy took off to Florida, and his lawyer called the police. I called my girlfriend who had had us over to dinner to tell her what happened. I only shared one thing with her—that I had had an orgasm. The police came that night and put up crime-scene tape. The forensic team went through my whole apartment. I forgot my parents were bringing Kimberly home after she had spent the weekend with them. I spotted my stepdad, and the detective told me he would fill him in. My stepdad said he would take both kids for the night. It was hours after everyone left.

The following day, my stepdad brought the kids back. He told me I deserved everything I got. What a bastard. I wanted to beat the crap out of him. I received a call from the detective to come down to the station. They brought me to a room and asked me again what happened that night. They asked, "Did you have an orgasm?" I said yes. They said the case was closed. That's why I hadn't wanted to go through this; I knew they would never believe me.

The treatment of rape then was nothing like it is now. Rape is rape. It doesn't matter if you know the person or not. No means no. Rape is an act of violence; you're violating someone's body and soul. There are a lot of different emotions and feelings going on inside you. That's the trauma of the rape, but it's a normal reaction to feel that way. I would be very careful when going out. Either finish your drink or have someone else watch it. Someone can slip a roofie in your drink, and you wouldn't even know it. It is odorless and colorless. All of these drugs can cause you to pass out and forget what happened. Then people can take advantage of you. That is what happened to me. I trusted someone who I thought was a friend. Back when I was sixteen, someone did that to me. That's why I was feeling dizzy and sick and passed out and didn't remember anything. Someone slipped something into my drink. If you have been raped, there are places out there today where you can go for help. Rape is no joke. It was just so unfair and another excruciating thing I had to go through.

After that episode, I had to move. I could not stay in a place where someone had violated me. So the three of us moved to an apartment in Brightwaters, New York. I was finally called to get Section 8 housing through the Town of Babylon. It helps low-income families with their rent. It was a big help. I would never have been able to afford rent on my own. Then Kimberly started school there. Kimberly was in second grade, and Michael was four. Through a friend, I got a job paid off the books. I told my boss that I had just moved into a new apartment and had no furniture. He had furniture made up for me. I thought it was so nice of him. Then I really needed a car to get back and forth, and my credit was no good, so he was my cosigner. I thought this man came from God.

Who would do this for me? I found out why the hard way. I was a very naive girl. One day, it was really hot in the back of the building where the guys work. He let them go early, and I had to stay. He had another office that was just his. He called me to that office. I went in, and he pushed me around so that my back was facing toward him; he pushed me up against the desk, pulled my pants down, and put his penis inside me. He said he was going to show me how to have sex. He said that was the reason why I didn't have a man. He was going to show me how to have sex to get a man. I couldn't wait to get out of there. I went home and called a friend and told her what happened. I didn't want to go back, but I needed the money, and what about the car? She told me to make a picture, put it on the wall, and yell at it. It was supposed to be him. I went to work the next day and told him how I felt, but one thing kept leading right back to having sex with him. I felt so gross. But I really I needed a job. I didn't know what to do. I also had this car that belonged to both of us.

I actually met this new maintenance guy at my apartment complex. One day, we started just bullshitting. I thought Harry was cute. The next day I saw him in an apartment with a girl and child. They were pretty friendly, and I figured he was married. Again I saw him and told him what I saw. He said it was his ex-girlfriend and that they had a child together, but they weren't together anymore. So one night I saw him outside, and he asked if he could come up. I said yes. We talked for hours lying on my bed. We started seeing each other. I was happy I had met him, because then my boss stopped bothering me. He wanted his parents to meet me, so one day he took me there to have dinner. It was his mom, dad, and sister. He told me that his mom was very sick with cancer. I did not know what to do. I felt terrible. It wasn't going to be long before she would die. She was a very nice lady. I felt bad for his sister, so I would take her out from time to time. When Harry and I went out, it would be to a bar. I wasn't crazy about hanging out at bars. I saw that he was drinking a lot, but I left it alone. When we first had sex, his mother told me that he told her I was a cold fish. I was embarrassed. I tried so hard to make him happy. He actually asked me to marry him.

We bought an engagement ring, and I was so excited. I wanted to surprise my parents with a surprise twenty-fifth wedding anniversary party. Now that I had a man, my boss stopped bothering me for sex. But he was helpful with the party. He knew the owner of the restaurant and helped me pay for everything, except the extras. I invited my aunts and uncles. I took the microphone and told everyone that Harry and I were engaged. They were so happy for us. They thought he was such a nice guy.

When the party was over, we went back to the apartment and carried the kids up the stairs. As we went to close the door, this fat little bitch walked in and grabbed me. She asked me what I was doing with her boyfriend. I was so out of it. I asked Harry what the hell was going on. Then I called the police and they arrested Harry, not her. He told me to come to the Riverhead court and get him out. I called "Mother" and told her I needed one hundred dollars to get him out. I thought it was because of what had just happened. When I got to the court, he told me there was a warrant out for his arrest for something. I can't remember. I was so upset but thought we'd get through it. At that time, my girlfriend had an apartment and let us rent it. But things seemed to get worse with Harry. He would come home whenever he felt like it. He was always at the bar and coming home drunk. One night, he told me he was going somewhere, so I followed him to the bar and waited and waited. When he came out, I saw him with a girl. He left, and I went after him with my car. He knew it was me and kept trying to get away from me with his car. Then he stopped. We both got out and started screaming at each other. I told him to get his ass home. I called his parents, and his mom said, "Don't marry him, he's an alcoholic." I thought I loved him, but it was just infatuation. I didn't listen, and a few days later, we were married. The reverend came to the house. I think we were married three months when I got a divorce. I found out he was with his baby's mother. After all that, my parents told me they were getting divorced. I gave them this awesome party, and now they were divorcing. I guess it really didn't come as a surprise. Like I said, they never had the greatest marriage.

But I also did it so they would love me. I know it sounds crazy, but that is all I ever wanted. So I figured that by giving them this party, it would make everything better. "Mother" went her way, and my stepdad went his way. We never heard from him again. Throughout this story, you see that most of the men I have been with were alcoholics. They say that most women will go with a man who is just like their father. I tried to reach my stepdad once in 2010 to try to have some kind of relationship with him. But that ended quickly, because he asked why I couldn't get along with my sister. I wasn't going to go through that whole thing again. He knew my sister and I had had no relationship growing up. By then, I knew where I stood. I had to stay away from him too.

CHAPTER 9

HAD THIRD CHILD

My two children and I moved into a beautiful three-bedroom house. The landlord owned every house on the block. I became close with the landlord and his wife, and they told me that the house was paid for and I could have it when they passed away. I did a lot of work on the house. Then I started working for a place called Home Products. They made steel sheds. I worked with three older men, and I was the receptionist. Even though they were much older, there was one in particular who was very handsome and nice to me. We talked every day, and I got to know him. I invited Jerry to go to the circus with the kids and me, because I had an extra ticket. We went and had a nice time. I don't remember why, but he spent the night. He slept on the couch, and I slept in Kimberly's bed. But I couldn't sleep and saw that he was still up, and we talked and then he made a pass to kiss me. He was very gentle and caring. We started dating, and he treated all of us like we were his family. He treated my kids like they were his own, and they loved him. It might be a problem for someone else that he was thirty years older than me, but he treated me better than all the younger guys. There was one big problem; he was married but had been separated for twenty years. His daughter accepted us, but not his son. Our situation wasn't the greatest, but it was better in many ways because he was nothing like the other men in my life. Jerry liked his scotch and his smoking. But when he got mad, he got a little nasty. I accepted it, because he wasn't hurting the kids or me. Jerry lived with us three nights a week and spent all day Saturday with us. When the kids had birthdays, or at Christmas, he treated them really well. He treated me like a princess. He wanted to marry me, but his ex would not give him a divorce. She thought he had money that she would get when he died. He didn't have anything but what he made weekly. He did buy me an engagement ring, and he ordered me a custom-made diamond cross. No man has ever done anything like that for me. In return, I treated him very well. On one special occasion, I bought him a silk robe. I had rose petals on the floor, leading to the bedroom. I'd written a special note and asked him to bring the wine glasses to the room, and we had wine and made passionate love. I was surprised when Jerry wondered if he could get me pregnant. He was sixty-two years old. He said he wanted a baby with me. He said that eating oysters helps in some way. They call it an aphrodisiac. So he would eat a lot of them. Then I was two months late with my period. I went to the store and did a test. It was positive. I couldn't wait to tell him. It didn't turn out the way I wanted it; it wasn't his night to stay over. I called him and asked him if he could come over because I needed to talk to him. He explained that he was tired and didn't want to.

I had to tell him over the phone. He was mad that I told him like that, but I couldn't wait another day. I had quit the shed place because I wasn't feeling well with my mitral valve prolapse. I was having chest pains and went to see a cardiologist. They did testing and found the mitro valve. Jerry gave me money every week plus he bought me and the kids things we needed. Things seemed to be moving along smoothly as I was getting bigger. Michael was still having issues but was very happy with Jerry.

On March 6, 1997, I was blessed with a baby boy. Jerry cried when he saw him. I did have complications during the labor. They could not find my cervix; it somehow ballooned up. I had to have an emergency C-section. That night, Jerry brought the kids to meet their new brother, Bobby. I was so excited that we were going to be an even bigger family, something I had always wanted as a little girl. At this point, I had been talking to my family, because I had a good man in my life. I asked my sister and her husband to be his godparents. I don't know why I did. I should have asked my best friend and her husband. Some things I never think through. There goes my impulsiveness again.

I started feeling very depressed. I thought I had the baby blues, but it was going on so long that I had to see a doctor. He put me on an antidepressant. Bobby turned one, and we had a party with Barney, the television character. Bobby was into Barney. Everything was Barney: his toys and his bedroom. But when Barney got there, he started running away. I guess Barney was just too big for him. We held Bobby, and Barney was playing with him, and then he played with the other kids. Jerry's daughter spent quite some time with the kids and us. But I never trusted her. She was always asking her father for money. Being the type of person he was, he would give it to her. She was never going to change. His older son didn't want anything to do with his new brother. He was cold and a spoiled brat. You'd think he would have been happy for his father.

When Bobby was two, we went to Sesame Place. We thought the kids would have fun there, and we all had a blast. All the Sesame Street characters were all over the place. They even had a parade, which was cool. We were exhausted and went back to the hotel. I had to drive about three to four hours back home the next day. We also went on a trip to Dorney Park the following summer; the kids were bigger now. We had a grand old time. It was such a big park. One side was rides, and the other was filled with water rides. The kids had the best time of their lives. I had to drive because Jerry didn't have a license. The kids had never gone away before, because I couldn't afford it on my own. For about three year's things were really good.

Then things stated going sour for Jerry and me. Bobby was having wild outbursts, throwing objects and running after us with knives. From the time he was two I knew he was different. He would not accept the word no for an answer. He was a little delayed in speech. I tried to take the pacifier away, but when I did, he would kick holes in the walls. I called early intervention, and they told me he would need speech therapy due to the pacifier. When he got older, I took him to a neurologist. The neurologists made me fill out a questionnaire. When the doctor walked in the room, he saw the way Bobby was acting with me, and he said he had oppositional defiance disorder and attention deficit hyperactivity disorder (ADHD).

Bobby didn't want to listen to what anyone had to say. They put him on Ritalin, but he was a zombie, so they changed it. His dad was getting older and wasn't in good health. He couldn't handle Bobby. He denied that Bobby had a disability, and he never worked with me. I would tell Bobby no, and his dad would buy him something. That wasn't helping the situation at all. I needed him on my side, but he was too old to be bothered. I had to put Bobby into a psychiatric hospital. They grabbed me outside and said that he would not stop screaming, so I had to take him home. He wasn't quite five yet. Not long after he turned five, I had to bring him back to the hospital, which was the hardest thing a parent could do. When we were driving in the car he would throw things at me or kick the windows. I was afraid he could knock me out or break the glass.

While I was leaving the hospital, I could hear him screaming for me. It just tugged at my heart. No parent wants to put her child in a hospital, but there was no other way to help him. I could have taken the easy way out and put my son in foster care; I didn't have to deal with all of this bullshit. He was allowed to come home for a day on the weekend to see how he would do, but he never did well. He still would not listen to me, and I would have to bring him right back. That was to try and teach him a lesson. A lesson! He couldn't care less. They would watch us interact. They would tell me what to do to try to help the situation. He was put on one medication after another.

There was no more that they could do for Bobby, so they sent him back home after a month. I tried to follow what they had taught me at the hospital, but it was hard. I signed him up for preschool. Bobby wasn't any better there; he was hurting other kids, throwing chairs, and jumping off tables. I thought the school would have thrown him out, but they didn't. They really hung in there with me. Bobby actually graduated from preschool and was ready for kindergarten. I was really nervous about that. The other kids were going through their own stuff. It wasn't easy for them. My attention was mostly spent on Bobby, and I did the best I could. Jerry was only coming on Saturdays. He couldn't put up with his son's behavior. There were times when we would be in the store and he'd want something. When I said no, he screamed bloody murder. People were looking at me like I was crazy. They didn't know what I was going through.

Kimberly was thirteen years old and wanted to know her father. I had called Robert and told him that his daughter wanted to meet him. I was very surprised when he said OK. He came over, they went out for lunch, and he took her school shopping.

Kimberly seemed happy. Her father came the following weekend, and he brought his wife and their daughter. After that, I don't know what was going through Kimberly's mind. One minute she was talking with her father, and then the next minute she wasn't. Bobby and Michael shared a room, which Michael hated. But I had my room, Kimberly needed her own room, and then there were the boys. I know Michael hated it, but there wasn't anything I could do. One day, while I was cleaning the house and started vacuuming, I turned the corner to see that Michael had shoved Bobby into a container and put the cover on it. If I hadn't seen that, Bobby would have been dead. Handling three kids with disabilities all by myself was just so overwhelming. Who do I take care of first? I know it was really hard on the other kids when Bobby took up most of my time. I had a nervous breakdown and wound up in the hospital. To get out, I had to talk to the doctor and take classes. I was told I was suffering from severe depression. Gee,

I wonder why? Then Jerry got sick with his heart, and he had to stop drinking and smoking if he wanted to stay alive a little while longer. He was put on all sorts of medication, which he hated. I did the best I could to take care of him. but soon Jerry was no longer in my life. I had to see a psychiatrist every month. Then my family's bullshit started again. We were no longer on speaking terms. What else was new? I didn't know whom to turn to.

Michael was now in third grade, and Kimberly was in fifth grade. The teachers always told me what beautiful children I had. But Michael's teacher would tell me he was very quiet and seemed withdrawn. They had him see the school psychologist. She was great, but Michael was hardly talking. It went on like this for years. Finally, when his sister started high school and Michael was still in middle school, the school psychologist suggested getting him therapy.

CHAPTER 10
THERAPIST FOR MICHAEL

We found a place on the outside. Through the town of Babylon that was free. They actually had a male therapist. I thought it was good for him to see a male. I took Michael to therapy once a week outside of school. After each session I would talk to Michael's therapist about things that were going on in our lives. Coincidentally, his name was Michael too. He would walk me out to the car, and I talked about Bobby's dad and other things. After a month, he asked if he could call me. I thought he was really cute. I gave him my number, and he said he would call late because he also went to night school. So the next night, he called me around 8:30 p.m. We talked for hours, like we had known each other for years.

After talking on the phone for weeks, Michael asked me out. He came to my house, and I drove us to this place called Babylon Bean Coffee House. We had coffee and a piece of cake. He also taught me how to play these cool card games. We had lots of laughs.

After about two hours, we went for a ride over by the docks. We just sat there and talked some more, and then we went back to my place. When he left, he never gave me a kiss. I was shocked. I figured he didn't like me. I called my girlfriend and told her. She told me that maybe he was just being a gentleman.

The next day, he called me again. I told him how surprised I was that he didn't kiss me. He said he was just being a gentleman. We made plans for that weekend to play cards with my friends. It was a lot of fun. They left close to midnight. Michael and I sat on the couch and started kissing. He told me I was beautiful that after having a third child I looked better than a girl in her twenties. I was already in my late thirties. That made me feel special. All of my kids got along well with Michael.

We went to a lot of baseball shows and baseball games. Michael and I went on a casino boat with his sister off Nautical Mile in Freeport, New York. It was my first time on a boat. I vomited the whole trip.

One night, I was over at his place, and he had this boat piece made out of glass with a candle inside it. I loved it. I asked him where he got it, and he said it was a gift. One day I wasn't feeling well, and he surprised me with one in a heart shape. It was so sweet of him. Then he asked me to take a ride. We ended up in Huntington on Main Street. We saw a craft fair and stopped. It wasn't great, so we got back in the car and started driving down Main Street. A song, "Kiss Me," came on the radio. I was singing it, and when I said kiss me, he leaned over and kissed me. I thought that was so romantic. We made one more stop at a country store, and I bought a little pillow to hang up.

One day when I was dropping Bobby off at school, he turned around and told me to wear my seatbelt. He knew I never wore it. He also told me to drive slowly. I said ok, but I thought it was a little strange. I did put my belt on. Eight minutes later, I was going down Main Street when a man making an illegal left turn hit me head-on. I must have blacked out for a second because I didn't realize what had happened. I had burn marks on my face and arms from the air bag. For a minute, I thought my son was psychic. It was like he knew what was going to happen.

Things were still crazy with Bobby. Bobby's kindergarten teacher told me about how he hurt one of the kids with a pencil. The teacher was very nice about it, but they could not have Bobby hurting any children. I had to put him into another hospital. It was so heartbreaking, but I didn't know what else to do. Bobby was in there for a few weeks.

The one good thing is that they had school there, so he didn't miss out on anything. They recommended putting him into a group home. The staff at the home went to classes to learn how to deal with these types of children. Bobby was in for about a year, but he was allowed to come home on weekends. I also had to learn how to deal with him. I had had another breakdown. I asked my half-sister to watch Michael and Kimberly. I asked Bobby's dad to watch him, since I was going into the hospital. Michael and I went out the night before I went into the hospital. He went into a card shop while I waited outside. Now, mind you, his dad was very sick. When he came out of the store, he started crying. I put my arm around him and asked if it was his dad. His dad had cancer and didn't have that much time to live.

He said he was going to miss me and he loved me. I spent the night by him and got up before him. The next day, I left little love notes around. "Mother" insisted on taking me to the hospital. I was so anxious, especially with her there. While we were waiting, Michael surprised me. He kissed me and said he would see me after work. When the doctor came in, she saw how I was shaking and gave me a sedative. "Mother" started in on a story about something that happened when she was sixteen. She always started in on that story with everyone. What was her deal with that? The doctor told her to be quiet and that she needed to leave.

They had someone ask me a lot of questions and do some kind of puzzles and paperwork. I got paid for it too. But by doing that they discovered that I was suffering with bipolar depression. Bipolar is a disorder where you have mood swings, depression, impulsiveness, and poor judgment. They explained to me that because of the sexual and physical abuse, I was being sexually destructive. I thought that if I gave men what they wanted, they would want me. They put me on a mood stabilizer and a new antidepressant. It was hard to hear that I had mental illness. There has always been such a big stigma against mental illness. But I was happy I had a name for what was wrong with me. I had feelings of hopelessness and despair. I had thought it would be better if I were dead. When you suffer from depression, even when you're on medications, it can take over your daily living. It's hard to get out of bed. You feel terrible pain throughout your body. You feel so alone. No one understands what you're going through. I had made several suicide attempts. When you're feeling like this, you must push yourself and say enough is enough. You have to get yourself some help. You need to see a therapist so that you have someone to talk to and a psychiatrist for medication. Sometimes it's not enough. So they try different ones until they find the right mixture. When I went for help, I realized there are millions of people who are depressed in some way. Some are not as bad as others. Bipolar disorder is a little different. You have mood swings. You're either up, or you're down. You are very impulsive, not just with shopping but also with making rational decisions. You don't think them through. We just want to be loved by someone. Some people steal, and some sleep with different men.

For the most part, I can control it with a mood stabilizer and an antidepressant. But medication doesn't always help to control it. I can still have symptoms. I still have a lot of impulses, but I can tell when I'm feeling impulsive and talk myself through it. Or I just stay home. When I feel impulsive, I want to go shopping, but I have to stay away or I will go bankrupt. That has happened to me before. I have seasonal bipolar disorder. I get more depressed during the winter months and sometimes during the late spring.

Michael came almost every day to see me in the hospital. After two weeks, I was sent home. It was Easter weekend, so Michael and I decided to pick up the kids. We got to my half-sister's house, and everyone was so silent. I asked how the kids were doing. No one would say anything. Then I saw my daughter in a dress that was low cut, with her boobs hanging out. Inside I was saying to myself, she's only fifteen. They were always treating her like she was an adult. So I started to leave and put my hand on my daughter's arm, and my half-sister said she was not going anywhere. She started an altercation with me and punched me in the face, and she told Michael and me to get out of her house. I called the police and explained to them what was going on. They said my daughter was telling my family that there was no food in the house and that I wouldn't let her get her ears pierced. As we were getting into the car, my sister was yelling that she was calling CPS on me, which stood for Child Protective Services. I can't begin to tell you how many times my family called CPS on me. They loved to start altercations for no reason. They wasted not only the worker's time but also time for someone who could have really used their services. All cases were unfounded. We went to pick up Bobby on the way home. I found out his father had found someone through the penny saver to watch Bobby all week. How could a parent do that without knowing the person? My son was acting so timid when he came home. I don't know what these people did to him.

That pissed me off royally. When we arrived home Kimberly would not talk to me. Thank God they hadn't gotten to Michael. The following day, a lady showed up at my door from Child Protective Services. She was really nice. She told me that she got a call that I had multiple personalities and that I had no food in the house. She spoke to both of my children separately. Even though she wasn't supposed to, she told me that it was my family who called on me. She said my family sounded like they were the crazy ones. She looked in my cabinets and refrigerator and said there was no case. It would be unfounded. After the woman left, I looked into what bipolar disorder meant.

While reading all these books, I realized that bipolar disorder is hereditary. When "Mother" was acting strange all those years, they called it manic-depressive. Now I had it and passed it on to my children. I felt bad that they had to suffer from it too.

Somewhere along the generations way back, someone had it and it carried on. I had this thing with Michael where every once in a while I would break up with him just to test him, to see if he would come back. He wanted to get married and have a baby of his own, but I told him I was almost forty. I was not going to have another child.

Since I had other children with mental illness, I didn't want to take that chance. I couldn't go through that again. Before we could get married, he wanted to be free and clear of bills, so we could have a decent life together. We were together three and a half years, and they were wasted years. Things changed because I wouldn't have another child. After three and half years we parted.

CHAPTER 11

BACK IN HOSPITAL

I ended up back in the hospital. Because of the insurance, I only got to spend a week there. All they did was change my medication. After the hospital stay, they wanted me to go into a program. I wish I could remember the name of it. It was for people who suffered from all types of mental illness. They would have classes to educate you on your illness. It was a half-day program. I met a few girls there, but they were really bad and screwed me so many times. I had to get them out of my life. Then, one day, while sitting in class, this guy sat across from me and smiled. I thought he was pretty cute, but I had to leave early. The next day, I came back, and he introduced himself as Rich. Rich and I hit it off, and I invited him over for dinner one night. He didn't have a car, so I picked him up at the train station. He had brought dessert, my favorite: éclairs. We had a really nice evening. We started seeing each other, and after four months he came to live with me. The kids were ok with him, but not like they were with Jerry and Michael. After another four months, Rich asked me to marry him. He told me he was married before and had a son about the same age as Kimberly.

Supposedly, his marriage hadn't worked out because he was never home. He worked a lot, and he and his wife hardly saw each other. Rich introduced me to his family. His parents were the nicest people. He had a brother and sister. His parents were happy for us but a little concerned. They knew Rich a lot better than I did. Rich bought me a princess engagement ring. It was beautiful. Rich knew I was seeing a therapist who felt I might have been sexually abused as a child. She wanted me to have hypnosis and had a connection with a professional, so she sent me to her. Rich and I went a few times. They wanted me to try to remember things on my own. I only remembered the color black. When I went back to my therapist, she wanted me to listen to the tape that the hypnotist made of me talking about what happened. She said that it wasn't going to be easy to hear. On the tape, the hypnotist said for me to go to a safe place. I was on the beach, and it was a beautiful day. I said I had seen a door, and she told me to open it. I said no; I was afraid. She said she was right next to me, and nothing was going to happen. It was really dark, and she told me she had a flashlight, and she turned it on. All I saw was a bunch of doors. There was one door that I wanted to open, but I was petrified. She again told me it was ok. She was with me, and she turned the flashlight on. We turned the knob together. The room was completely black. Then she shone the light inside. There was a man, dressed in black, standing over a crib with an infant in it. You do not want to know what that man was doing to that baby. Use your imagination. That man was my biological father.

That night, I just kept going over and over in my mind what happened. I was hurting. Rich was in the kitchen, and I was in the bedroom. I took one of his box cutters from work and slit my wrists. I just sat there, and Rich walked in a fury. He put towels on my wrists and took me to the hospital. Rich had called "Mother," which I did not know. She said she wanted to be there for me. Where was she when I needed her all of my life? Now she wanted to be with me. I came right out and asked her if she knew about what he had done. Maybe that was why she hated him so much. She told me she had an inkling. She had an inkling and did nothing about it. What kind of mother was she? She was not sympathetic at all. I wanted to put my hands around her throat.

My therapist told me to confront my father so I could have some kind of peace. After I came out of the hospital, I called the phone directory and asked for Bob. They gave me his number. I looked it up and found out where he lived. I told Rich and "Mother" that I wanted to go and confront him. They agreed. I said I wanted to immediately. I don't know why "Mother" came; maybe she wanted some justice. I had the confidence, so I had to do it right then. We drove to Mannituck and pulled up in front of the house. I had to wait awhile before I was ready. I first made a call. It wasn't his third wife who answered. I asked for Bob. She asked who was calling, and I said it was his daughter, Agnes. I heard her put her hand over the phone. Then she came back on and said that he doesn't have a daughter Agnes. She hung up the phone. I took a deep breath and walked to the front door and knocked. Bob answered and saw me. I started to say something, and he pushed me away and closed the door. I just yelled outside, "You son of a bitch, how could you sexually abuse your child?" I couldn't take any more, so I got in the car and went back home. It wasn't the satisfaction I wanted, but it was the best I could get. I had to try to go on with my life.

"Mother's" brother, my uncle, was dying of cancer, so I wanted to have the wedding before he died, and we made it three months earlier. We had it at a small restaurant, not big at all. Just a few close friends and family. At this point, "Mother" was back in my life. "Mother" was in and out of my life, all my life. I kept trying to make things work, but I had to get rid of the negativity. When I tried on my dress to show her, she cried. "Mother" said, "You're finally getting married." She would only be in my life if I were married. She really liked Rich. She would tell me that when he looked at me she could tell how much he loved me. We were getting all the final touches done when a situation arose. Michael was still having problems. The school psychologist and I kept in close contact. I would drive the kids to school when they were in the same school. Kimberly was now in high school. The elementary school was about five blocks away. The school psychologist said that Michael could walk to school.

When it was time to go to school, Michael was begging me to bring him. I told him he could walk. Rich and I literally had to push him out the door. Then we heard Michael throwing rocks at the window. I called the psychologist and told her what was going on. While I was in the bedroom on the phone, Rich was getting upset because he could break the windows. I heard Rich tell Michael to get in the house, and then Rich came in the room while I was still on the phone talking to the psychologist. All of a sudden, Michael came in with a huge knife and tried to stab Rich. I got in front of Rich. Michael came within inches of stabbing me. I was screaming into the phone, and the psychologist heard everything and called the police. I knew Michael wouldn't hurt me, but I didn't know why he came at Rich like that. The police came and handcuffed my boy. I was mortified and felt such anguish for Michael. We had to follow the police to the hospital, the same one Bobby once stayed at. Michael wasn't a bad boy, but it was for everyone's protection.

My life was a living nightmare. My poor kids had to suffer with the same illness I had. It just wasn't fair. Michael was diagnosed with bipolar disorder and came out of the hospital on a mood stabilizer. He was not crazy about being on medication. Rich wanted us to move into a new place together. So I lost the house the landlord was going to give me. We found a house in Farmingdale. Rich worked nights at Pathmark and would drive my car, even though he didn't have a license. Sometimes I would take him to work and pick him up in the morning. Our day was finally arriving. On Saturday, I wanted to go shopping. So Rich, the kids, and I spent a few hours out. When I got home and opened the door, everyone yelled "Surprise!" My half-sister was throwing me a little bridal shower. My two aunts, my cousin, Rich's parents, and "Mother" were there. It was a shock that my half-sister would do this for me. I had asked her to be my maid of honor, because my friend pulled out at the last minute. It was really nice to see everyone, especially my aunts and cousin, who I hadn't seen in God knows how long. After I opened my presents, Rich's parents told us we could still call it off. Our wedding was the following Friday. I was stunned by what they said. I just had to let it go. But the next week, there I was, getting into my wedding dress, waiting for the limousine. The limousine pulled up, and I started crying. I could not believe this day was here. I was getting married. The limousine pulled up right in front of the door, and I came walking in. Everyone was so happy. Rich had a big smile on his face. We also wrote our own vows. What Rich wrote was the most beautiful thing about being a family. I also talked about him coming into our lives, and my children having a father, and how lucky I was. After we were done, we got into the limo and headed for the restaurant at Singletons. We had to wait for them to do the last finishing touches. Then they introduced us as Mr. and Mrs. Rich McGee. His son made a beautiful speech, and so did my daughter. Then she sang us a song, "Wind beneath My Wings." My daughter had a beautiful voice, and I cried like a baby. But Rich seemed to be acting strange and didn't seem to be into it.

After it was over, we went to stay at a Marriott for the night. "Mother" watched the kids for me, which was shocking. She really never could stand the boys, especially Bobby. She did not want to understand what he was going through. At the hotel I put on a sexy nightie, but all Rich wanted to do was sleep. We never had sex. I felt embarrassed and uncomfortable. This was now my husband. Why, after all this time, did he act this way?

The next morning, we got up, and I said I couldn't believe we were husband and wife. He was like, yeah. We went to a diner, had breakfast, and headed home. I had to relieve "Mother." We said our hellos to the kids, and then we sat in our room, opening up the envelopes people gave us. "Mother" gave us nothing. I know she didn't have much, but something would have been nice. We ended up with about $7,000. That was a nice surprise.

The next day, I thought everything went back to normal. Rich went to work, and the kids went back to school. Kimberly was in Rosemary High School. That day, I got a call from the principal. He said that Kimberly told a friend she had tried to hang herself that morning. She put a towel around her neck and hung it on the door. I was sleeping in the next room, and I was knocked out from my medicine. Her neck was all red. I called Rich and told him to meet us at Brunswick Hospital. Kimberly was answering all the questions the nurse was asking her. I had to find out that she was doing drugs and that she just wanted to kill herself. I could not believe what was happening. I had to stay with her all night until they got her a room the next day. All she was doing was cursing at me, pushing me away as I was trying to comfort her. The nurse kept telling her to stop and that I was her mother. She couldn't care less.

I went back the next day to visit her and bring her some things. She wanted nothing to do with me. My marriage with Rich was falling apart. He was working a second job at 7-Eleven in the evening. I would walk around the corner and visit him, and he was always on the phone. When he saw me, he would hang up. I had my concerns that he might be having an affair. Our sex life wasn't the greatest. One evening, we were having dinner when Rich slammed his hand on the table and told Michael to eat right. I got so upset that he was yelling at my son like that. I froze for a moment and then threw a bowl of peas over Rich's head. It was quiet for three minutes, and then everyone started laughing.

One night, I decided to take a ride to his job. I sat far enough away that he couldn't see me. He must have come out on his break with this girl, and they were kissing. What a blow that was. I went back home and tried to sleep, but I couldn't. I was thinking about how I was going to confront him. I confronted him the following morning. I never told him I was spying on him, and he denied the affair completely.

From there, things got worse. When Kimberly came home from the hospital, she treated me like shit. I asked her to let me in her room so we could talk. She kept saying no. I kept asking her to please open the door. Rich came over and asked her if he could talk to her, and she let him in. They were in there for thirty minutes. I told him that was enough and to come out. I tried the door and it was locked. I kept yelling for him to come out. Then the door opened; she ran downstairs, and he followed her. I didn't like the way they acted with each other, and neither did his parents. I didn't know if something was going on between the two of them. I asked them both to come upstairs, saying that enough was enough. He started cursing at me and called me a cunt. I don't know where it came from, but I guess I had had enough with men. I told him to get the fuck out of the house. I grabbed garbage bags and started throwing his clothes in them. He was still cursing and came up to me, chest to chest, like he was going to hit me. He told me he couldn't take the kids anymore. He grabbed the bags and walked out. He came back the next day with his girlfriend to get the rest of his stuff.

In April 2003, I had gotten a contested divorce. It cost me $350, but it was over. Now it was time for the kids and me to move on. We left that place and moved into a quaint little house in Bellmore, New York. I signed the kids up for school. Michael went into a Boces program that helped special needs children. Kimberly started high school. After a while, she was put into a high school Boces program at Rosemary Kennedy because she was having difficulties. Now that my daughter turned sixteen, she was going out whenever she felt like it, and she would come home in the wee hours of the night. She hung out with these boys and this one girl who got her involved in drugs. She was having sex with different guys. I had to get a PINS petition, person in need of supervision. That was a joke. The probation officer didn't do anything. She was in a program that helped older children with things they were going through. She was supposed to be helping Kimberly, but Kimberly did what she wanted to do, and she didn't care about anyone but herself. Kimberly was diagnosed with bipolar disorder and borderline personality disorder.

That's a part of the reason why she was acting the way she was. To see another child in handcuffs just tore my heart apart. She had to go in front of the judge. He told her she could either behave or go into a group home at Modern Heights. I knew what that place was like, and it wasn't for her. She would probably come out worse. Kimberly was allowed to come back home with me. I called her father, Frank, and explained the situation. He was strict, and I thought she really needed that. I asked him if she could live with him. He said yes, that he would straighten her out. I needed some kind of help, and the boys really needed my attention. Kimberly had called me and asked to come home. I told her no. About a week later, instead of talking to Frank, Kimberly manipulated me once again. She told me her father had pushed her into a metal chair, and she had bruises on her neck. Of course I went running and picked her up. She had some little bruises, but I wasn't sure what to believe. After talking to Frank, he said it was an accident, and she was trying his patience. I believed him, because I knew my daughter all too well. She wouldn't do what she was asked to do. When my daughter got in trouble, she always blamed everyone else but herself. That's what borderline personality disorder is. She called her worker and told her what happened, and they called Child Protective Services on her father. I knew Frank was really going to freak out, which he did. He told me that he never wanted to see her again. I honestly understood him. The case was unfounded, thank God. I also knew what he went through, because my family called CPS on me so many times, and those calls were all unfounded. I know they were trying to prove something. What's that saying? What goes around comes around. My family was all over me because I had children out of wedlock. My half-sister would always say she had the best kids. Well, her child isn't so perfect. He got his girlfriend pregnant, and now they have a baby. But that is ok in their eyes. They are not so perfect after all.

Jerry eventually came back into our lives, which was great. Not that he really ever left, because he saw Bobby every Saturday. He would gamble every day on Lotto and instant tickets. He would win $250 or $500 here and there. Then he would take us to New York City to the Museum of Natural History and out to beautiful restaurants.

We would also go to Atlantis Marina. I knew it was time for us to move again. I couldn't deal with the bullshit anymore. I figured if we moved away from here, Kimberly might get better. So we moved to an apartment in Rockaway Queens. We were there only five months, because my landlord would not sign the Section 8 lease. Now we had to move again. Kimberly had been seeing a guy who was doing some drugs. Because of Kimberly's illness, she wasn't making the right choices. She had told me that she didn't get her period. I asked her if they used condoms. She said yes, but I don't think they did. We got a pregnancy test, and it came back positive. I was going to be a young grandma. Her boyfriend and the boys were waiting in the living room to find out the results. She came out with this big grin on her face, saying she was pregnant, and I couldn't believe I was going to be a grandma. I would never do what my mother did to me. I was going to be there for my daughter.

We had to start looking for another place. I found a house in Franklin Square, New York. I had the whole house, and there was an apartment upstairs. Kimberly and her boyfriend were living in a one-room shack in my uncle's yard. I gave my daughter a baby shower in the backyard. Nine months had gone by so fast. My daughter gave birth to a baby boy. He was absolutely beautiful. I was at their place, spending time with the baby and cleaning up the place. I found out that the girl above me was moving out, so I told my daughter that maybe they could move up there. This way, they had me there if they needed any help.

Kimberly's husband had gotten a good job working for Cablevision. It would be a little tight, but it was better than what they were living in. So they moved in. I was in my glory with my grandson right there. Things were going really well. I had given my grandson a baptismal party. Kimberly's best friend and her older brother were the godparents. I was sitting at the table with all of my girlfriends. We were watching the baby's grandfather on Kimberly's husband's side take the three-month-old baby and throw him up in the air. The baby kept spitting up. All my friends were talking about what an idiot he was for doing that. But they let it go because they didn't want to start anything. The following morning, Kimberly came down at six o'clock in the morning and put my grandson next to me.

She would say, "Grandma." So I would take over and clean him up and feed him. She confided something to me. She said that her boyfriend got frustrated with the baby last night and kind of shook him. She asked me if I thought he was ok. I checked him over, but I offered that she should take him to the doctor just to make sure. I don't know if she did. She told me she did and that everything was good. That night, I was going to a parent's group for children with special needs. I mentioned what happened to my grandson. Everyone was concerned, but our talks went on.

The following day, I got a call from the supervisor. She told me she was required to call Child Protective Services. I did not know that. I told my daughter, and she asked why I had to talk about her business. I told her it just came up in conversation. It wasn't done on purpose. When her boyfriend came home from work, she told him what happened. He cursed me out and told me to stay the fuck away. It wasn't a good situation. My daughter wasn't the same toward me. A few weeks later, I heard them opening their door and walking up the stairs when I heard something go bump, bump. I heard the two of them say, "Oh shit, we forgot to lock the infant seat," and the baby fell out. They were too young to have a baby. They weren't mature enough. I hated to do what I had to do. But I wasn't doing it to hurt them; he was my grandson. I had to call CPS to protect my grandchild.

They were young to have a child. Everyone— "Mother," my half-sister, and his family—hated me for what I did. No one talked to me anymore. My daughter and her boyfriend moved out. I did not see my grandson for quite some time. I eventually moved back to West Babylon. My daughter was telling me she was moving to North Carolina soon. I did not want to be away from my grandson and decided to move there with them. My daughter would talk to me when she felt like it. She was in my life, and she would go out of my life. She was just like "Mother." Even when we weren't talking, I was always trying to reach out to her. I would send her birthday cards and holiday cards. I would try to talk to her on social media. But it was always on her terms.

CHAPTER 12

OUT OF STATE

We happened to go first. We moved to Wilmington, North Carolina. It was very different from New York. My daughter never moved to North Carolina, so we were left alone down there. Michael did not want to move there, so he asked his sister if he could live with her. She said yes. About a month later, Michael called me to tell me that he was living on the streets. His sister threw him out. Kimberly was not moving to North Carolina. I could not have my son living that way. So I drove twenty-four hundred miles round-trip to New York and picked him up. I know he wasn't happy in North Carolina. I wasn't too thrilled with it either. We would find needles and pot pipes. The cops came around all the time.

They weren't equipped for children with disabilities. I went home to New York to spend Thanksgiving with friends, and I asked my daughter if we could stay with her for a few days. She told me she had no room, so we had to sleep in our car. When my friend found out, she told me to stay with her. She was really pissed at my daughter for not taking her mom and siblings in. We stayed for two days and then drove back to North Carolina. I had put an ad on Craigslist asking if anyone had a place for rent in New York. I got an e-mail that someone had a house in Shirley, New York. We came back to New York to meet the landlord and make sure everything worked out. A couple of days later, we drove back to New York to get the keys. It was a little house, but it was just right for the boys and me. They always had to share a room, but they were older now, so it was a little easier. But Shirley was way out in the boondocks. It was a forty-five-minute ride to see my friends or Jerry. Sometimes he came to us. I fixed it up nice; I painted and put rugs down, and I cleaned up the yard, which was a lot of work. No one came to see us because we were so far away. I felt so alone. My daughter and I started talking again. My grandson was turning two. I threw a little party for him, because I was not allowed to be at the parties my daughter gave. "Mother," my half-sister, and our oth-er family were more important than me. My daughter said that's the way it had to be. It was her choosing. That's how my daughter treated me.

She would rather have everyone else and not her mom. Everyone was always putting shit in her head about how I was not a good mom, but it had been that way since she was a little girl. They had brain-washed her. I was no good because I had put my son in hospitals and group homes, and she never wanted anything to do with him. They did not live my life, so they couldn't understand what I was going through. Instead of being there for me, they were against me.

CHAPTER 13

TOO FAR AWAY FROM EVERYONE

We were so far away from everyone that we had to move again. This time it was to North Babylon, New York. It wasn't the greatest place for people like us.

Bobby still had issues, but he was put into a program. The child's parent was assigned another parent to be there for them. They would have support groups for the parents and children. They wanted to get the children to learn to socialize with one another. But that never worked out for Bobby; he wanted to hang around me. Bobby wasn't that bad, but he still needed guidance. I have never given up on my children. I would find ways to get them the help they needed. At this point, Jerry was becoming very ill. He had to be put on dialysis, and his heart wasn't well.

Jerry was in the hospital. I went there every day like I was his wife. I would clean him and shave him, and I would bring him the food he wanted. Then he ended up in a therapeutic home, which he hated, and he had to stay there for about three weeks. On weekends, he was allowed out. Bobby and I would pick him up and go out. He was now grouchy and older. I understood how he felt, but he was constantly yelling at me for stupid things. One day, Bobby said, "Daddy, please stop yelling at Mommy." At that point, I realized that I couldn't see him for a while. I needed a break. He never tried calling Bobby. This really hurt me, and I'm sure Bobby was feeling it too.

Bobby went back into another group home in Merrick, New York. He constantly asked me if he could come home, and I would have to explain why he couldn't. I had to move out of North Babylon into a one-bedroom apartment because that's the way Section 8 worked. I moved into a senior citizens' complex. It was pretty nice. I always liked hanging around older people. Bobby would come home on weekends. One weekend, it was Bobby's thirteenth birthday. We had a little something for him.

The following day, I was on Facebook, and I saw that his daughter had written to me to tell me that Jerry had passed away. I read it, and the tears starting flowing down my cheeks. She told me he had passed away on Bobby's thirteenth birthday. The hardest thing was going to tell Bobby. They let me tell him at the group home. This way, there were people there if he needed them. He didn't show any emotion. He just sat there, taking it all in. He didn't want to talk about it, so we left him alone.

When and if he was ready, he could come and talk to me. Michael, Bobby, my friend, and I all went to the service. Even though I wasn't talking to my daughter, I contacted her on social media to let her know. When we were in the church, I turned around and saw Kimberly and her husband in the back. Jerry's son had him cremated, which surprised me because Jerry told me he wanted to be buried. After the service, they did a gun salute for him because he was a veteran. Jerry told me that Bobby would get the flag, but his older son took it. Jerry was so afraid of upsetting his son that he never told him anything. He lied to me. Then we wanted to pick up the stuff that we had given to Jerry to store from his house, and we were told that they had thrown it all out. What a disgrace. His son was so ignorant.

A year went by quickly, and Bobby was allowed back home. Once again, I had to move to get a two-bedroom apartment. We moved back to Farmingdale. We were only living there a little while when Bobby went out of control. This time he was hurting me and putting holes in the walls. I called for help right away, I was so afraid of him. It's not a good feeling to be afraid of your own child. I put him into a different group home. Fortunately, they were right around the corner. I spent so much time over there going to therapy with Bobby. He would write me notes saying how sorry he was. After a year, Bobby came back home. The medication was really helping him, and I learned how to be sterner. He was also told that if he ever laid a hand on me again, it would be his last. He would not be allowed to come back home. Bobby seemed to be getting better and better, and he was maturing.

CHAPTER 14
LAST HOSPITALIZATION

The last time I was in the hospital was in 2009. I met another patient while I was there, and we have remained friends. I've never had a male friend in my life, and it's quite a different relationship from the ones I've had. I feel at ease with him. He is someone I can trust, and I don't trust many men. We were there for each other, helping each other with the situations we were both going through. It's nice to know I can finally have a relationship with a man. He is now remarried, and she knows all about me, and my friend and I talk to each other at least once a month.

After I left the hospital, I got a call from my half-sister, whom I hadn't spoken with in years. My half-sister said that my daughter and my two grandchildren were living with "Mother." She explained that things were bad between them and that Kimberly needed somewhere to go. She asked me if I would take her and the kids in. I told her I would. Where else were they going to go? My half-sister brought her, the kids, and all of their stuff to my place. My daughter thought she was a queen and stayed on the couch all day. I was running around, cleaning up after the kids. Kimberly had left her husband for another guy. They had all these plans of getting married, but he was an immature idiot. She and the kids would take the train and go to his place. It was great having my grandchildren, even though I didn't know the youngest one at all.

My half-sister would call me every day, talking about my daughter and her bullshit. Then my daughter would be talking to my half-sister whispering. "Mother" got involved, and I figured life is too short. So I let bygones be bygones.

After a week, my half-sister said she was taking my daughter and the kids to Hicks Nurseries. I asked my half-sister if I could go with her, and she said yes. The following day, "Mother," my half-sister, my daughter, and the kids all got into her truck and left. No one said a word to me. About five hours later, they came back. No one knocked; they just walked into my place. "Mother" sat at one side of the dining room table and my daughter at the other. I was putting on my grandson's shoes to take him to the park. My family said no, that the children would be spending the night at "Mother's." I asked what the hell was going on. Michael was standing there with me.

My half-sister yelled, "What the fuck do you mean, what's going on here?"

I replied, "You walk in here. No one says a word, and now everyone is leaving."

There they went again, playing their little game. My half-sister brought my daughter to my house because she wasn't getting along with "Mother." And now she was going to spend the night there. What kind of bullshit was that? I felt bad for my grandkids, and it wasn't them I was kicking out. It was my daughter. I called her and told her to come get her things. I had already packed all their things and put them outside. I did not want them in my house.

My half-sister showed up with my daughter. She knew I was looking out the window and gave me the finger. What lowlifes they are. My son called my half-sister later and yelled at her for what she did. He saw everything and didn't know why they did what they did either. My half-sister started screaming that I was on welfare and a piece of shit. I wasn't on welfare; I was on social security disability. I told him just to hang up and let it go. At least I knew it wasn't just me. I would have said I was sorry, but something wasn't right. Kimberly's father told me that one day she would screw me just like she had screwed him. I told him he was right. My kids are my kids, and I'll do anything to help, but if you keep screwing with me, then that's it. I had to learn to forgive my daughter and move on with my life.

Often times the people who are closest to us, do not realize that they have hurt us; they may not always be sensitive to your needs. That's why I needed to depend on Gods inner strength to pull me through. I believe that God will someday bring me the man of my dreams. It will be on his time, not mine. It could be in a week, a month or a year, but I know he is out there waiting for me.

CHAPTER 15

MICHAEL

B y now 2013 Michael had moved out of the house to live with his girlfriend and her family. I'm so proud of him. He works at BJ's Wholesale Club and at a nursing home at night. He may not be perfect, but at least he's moving on in his life, working two jobs and with a girlfriend, soon to be fiancé. Even with his troubles, he's making a life for himself. I am very proud of him. He saved his money to buy his own car. He is doing his best, and that's all you can hope for when it comes to your kids. Bobby's behavior started getting bad again. He was starting to hurt me. He had such anger. He would still punch holes in the walls. I was so afraid of him. I had to call the police, and they put him in the hospital and changed his medication again. The doctors and counselors from the Single Point Of Access Program all decided to put him into another group home through a different program. It was good because he was only five blocks away from me, and it was easier to see him. They worked differently than all the other homes. The counselors there really helped him.

Bobby and I were working hard to make things better between the two of us. After a year, Bobby was allowed to come home. He came back in April 2011. We worked on our boundaries and how to talk to each other. I told him that if he ever touched me again, he would not be able to come back home.

Bobby is now eighteen and has graduated with a lot of help from me. Bobby is going to Barry Tech to be a mechanic technician. He has one more year and can start working in his field. I have been teaching him how to drive like I did with my other two children. He has been doing a great job. He drives every day. I wish I could buy cars for both of my sons, but I just can't. Bobby now is more self-confident, and it's the greatest thing to see. I will be getting Bobby his driving lessons so he will be able to drive and start learning to be self-sufficient. I had to save my son; I did not want to see him wind up in jail.

Even though Bobby knows that I do what I do to help him, he's still angry with me that he had to go into these places. But he doesn't understand that I did what I did to save him. He is the man he is today because of me. I hope that one day he will realize that. I sacrificed everything for my children. Although I have been through so much shit, I will never say I was perfect. Life has knocked me down many times. It has shown me things I never wanted to see, and I've experienced sadness and failures. But I always got back up, and tough times have made me a stronger person. It may have taken fifty-one years, but I have learned from my mistakes. I used to hold my head down, and now I hold my head up high. Everyone has flaws. I am no longer a victim. I have met many people in my life that have made positive impacts. Each time, I've learned something new from them. I have found friends from high school on social media, and they affirmed what I knew already. "Mother" was a bitch. They said they remembered "Mother" was always yelling at me, and they saw the beatings. They wished they could have done something, but back then there was nothing they could say that would change things. At least I had some confirmation that I wasn't going crazy.

My therapist told me that for my life to go on, I had to get rid of the negative people in my life. I did that. I no longer see "Mother," my half-sister, or my daughter. All I ever wanted was "Mother's" approval. I never got her blessing, but I have since found my destiny.

CHAPTER 16
MY LIFE TODAY

My first passion in life was to write. My second passion was to help people. I started volunteering at a nursing home, which gave me such gratification. I have made many friendships, and I still keep in touch with a very special lady. My heart goes out to her. She is so lonely and unhappy. I go and see her at least once a week and call her on the phone. I keep in touch with another woman whose husband is also in there. The four of us try to spend time together every Saturday. I feel like this one patient is the grandmother I never had. They are so lonely and depressed. She tells me that my visits make her day. I wish I could do so much more for them. The worst part is when they pass away. It breaks my heart. It's like losing a part of your family.

Since I had been volunteering there for a year I was told there was a position available. I was so excited. I would be working per diem in housekeeping. It was hard work. I had to clean the rooms and do the laundry, which was so gross. It smelled of piss and crap all over them. I was getting sick. My boss would constantly make sexy gestures towards me. He would call me in his office and would show me how hard he was for me. I was thinking to myself, "this can't be happening again". This went on for a month and I quit my job. I went to my psychiatrist and told her what happened. I could not get him out of my head while I was sleeping. I was so scared of him. She told me I was suffering from Post traumatic stress disorder. She gave me something to calm me down. I didn't want to tell my job what happened because I was afraid. The nursing home is only a few feet away from my home. I didn't want any kind of conflict with anyone. All the workers knew both of us. At the time I was hired so was another girl. I found out she quit the following week. They had to know something was up. I wouldn't leave my house till I knew he was gone for the day. After about four months he supposedly left that job. When I asked what happened to him they told me he got another job. Only they know the truth

Kimberly has not let me see my three grandchildren in five years, and I don't even know the other two girls. She thinks she's hurting me, but she's really hurting her children. One day, when they become of age and we find one another, they might resent their parents. Bobby now has a relationship with his sister. For Bobby, it's really about being able to see the kids. He has bonded with them, and he loves being an uncle. I'm happy for him, but I don't like it when they talk shit and put things in my grandkids' heads.

Michael hasn't had a relationship with his sister for about eight years. He was the smart one. He saw through the family and protected his mother. Bobby has always wanted a relationship with his sister. He was too young to know what was going on. I was afraid of her and my family poisoning him. So I wouldn't let him talk to or see her. When he was in the group home, he went on to social media to talk with her. I had the counselors see what they were talking about. Bobby had told her he was back in a group home, and she said to him that I was a bitch for putting him in there. First, she wasn't living in my home. Second, she knew what her brother was like all her life.

But now that he's eighteen, I can't stop him. He is really there for the kids. So my daughter is back in my life, but not physically. I thought that part was over. It's causing me such grief and heartache again, but I must continue going on with my life as I have. Bobby does not like conflicts, so he said he doesn't talk about me, and she doesn't talk about me. Bobby and I have a great relationship, even though he has some anger issues toward me. We sometimes go to the movies. We play jokes on each other. We have lots of laughs. It's the greatest feeling to finally have some type of bond with my son. We still have our moments where we get into arguments. His outlet is his sister. He needs a better outlet than his sister. He goes and stays with her every weekend. He doesn't have any friends. He still has problems socially. He has severe anxiety which stops him from doing a lot of things. He will not talk on a phone. He just wants to text. I am trying to teach him how to do things for when he goes out on his own. Even with a job he can't be inter-active with people. He has to work behind the stage sort of speak. You know I told him I could have easily given up on him and said here put him in foster care. I don't want to deal with it anymore. But I didn't do that. I will never give up on my son.

One day Bobby and I got into a serious argument. I didn't like what he was saying to me. He was be-ing disrespectful. He was going to his sisters. I told him then you might as well stay there and don't come back. We all say things in the heat of the moment. I decided to get a hold of my daughter on instant mes-sage through social media. I wanted to let her know what was going on. I was surprised when I heard from her. She said she was going to ask her landlord if Bobby could rent downstairs. So I said to her "he is going to stay with you?" She replied "yes". I told her what needed to be done so I could move on with my life. She told me he would have to follow her rules. Get a job and not sleep all day. After two weeks I get a text message from Bobby stating he is coming home. I texted him back permanently. He said I guess so. I was so confused. I messengered my daughter and asked what was going on. She said he didn't want to follow the rules. When he came home two days later we had a decent conversation. He told me he was going to do what she said. I told him that wasn't what she told me. I said I'm getting conflicting stories here. So I messengered my daughter telling her I was confused. Guess what? She never answered me. But Bobby told me he is going there every weekend. It makes no sense to me, but what am I going to do. Here go the games again and I'm not playing them anymore. I'm moving on with my life.

My therapist has read my manuscript to get a better understanding of what I have been through. We both came to the conclusion that maybe something happened to "Mother" when she was younger. Or maybe she changed because her best friend married my dad. Maybe she knew what my dad did to me and did nothing about it. I could make up excuses. They still would not give her the right to do what she did to me. I looked just like my father. Subconsciously, maybe she saw him through me and was beating him. She would tell me that if she ever saw him, she would stab him with a knife. I remember how I come home from my grandparents' house and she would cut the dresses my grandmother made for me. I could think of a million reasons why. But that does not give a parent a right to harm his or her child like that. It's sick, but unfortunately that's just the way it was. I had to pay for everyone's mistakes. To this day "mother" has not called me. She has never apologized. That's ok. I'm fine with it now. "Mother" was never a strong person. She could never stick up for herself. When my half-sister's around she follows her around like a lost puppy. She had a mouth when she was beating and verbally abusive, but she can't stand up to anyone. I came out of all this as the strongest person. They say what doesn't kill you makes you stronger.

I just want to finally put it all behind me, once and for all. The best things to come out of all of this were my boys; those were the best days of my life. They are my world.

I want to tell you about a very special person in my life, Peggy, whom I met through Birthright. We still remain friends after twenty-five years. Peggy has been my spiritual adviser, friend, mother, and teacher. No matter what I did in those twenty-five years, she was never judgmental. She understands why I did what I did. Peggy has always praised me for being the mother that I am and has told me that I did the best I could. It took me a long time to realize that, thanks to her. I now know that I am a good mother. It took me twenty-five years to see it, but now I know. She always tells me that I persevere. She always gives me guidance and love. We talk on the phone and we have lunch every couple of months. I look forward to that. I can never thank her enough for getting me this far.

I went to a support group for parents of children with challenging disabilities. When I went there, so many people were going through the same things I was. It was nice to know I wasn't alone, to know I wasn't crazy. A lot of people were cruel to us because our children were different, and it's just a shame. My older son went to a Boces school where he became friends with three other boys. They had started their own rock band, and since my son didn't play an instrument, he was the singer. I thought it was great for him.

He was coming out of his shell. My son couldn't handle being different and didn't like being on medication. These kids just didn't like being different from other kids. They could not understand that it was a disease, just like having diabetes. They didn't like the side effects. It would make them get very heavy and have enlarged breasts. It didn't help their self-confidence. They never felt comfortable in their own skin. These are the reasons why I wrote my book, and also because it helped me therapeutically. I'm not saying I'm not going to have challenges anymore because I will. But I now know how to get through those trying times. Because of God and my spirituality, I have found peace. Joel Olsteen has become my savior. He has taught me how to be positive and get all that negativity out of me. He showed me how to get through the storms. Once that storm is over I have past my test and a new opportunity will come along. PSALM 17- 8, I know the Lord is always there with me. I will not be shaken for he is right beside me. I believe that everything happens for a reason. I got to meet Joel at his book signing. I felt blessed when he shook my hand. He is a wonderful person. The following day I had tickets to see him at the Night of Hope. It was the most amazing thing I had experienced. God puts certain people in our lives at certain times. Today, I am best friends with Dave from high school, the one who wanted to go out with me back then. After thirty-some years, we found each other on social media, and now we are the best of friends. We get together for lunch or a movie, and for the first time I actually have a man in my life who isn't a bad guy. He is married with a beautiful family, and we treasure our friendship. He turned out to be a wonderful man, and I'm sorry I lost my chance, but at least I have his friendship. We are there for each other through good and bad times. I know that he was put in my life for a reason. It's funny how things work out. I also have met a few other friends on social media that I've gone out with. It's the greatest thing to have friends. I'm finally living my life and doing what I want to do. I always gave my kids everything with what money I had. I never thought about me. Almost a year ago I sat in my therapist office and said "you know I bought myself some cloths and I feel guilty". She said "it's because you were always giving to your kids or someone else". She said I have to keep doing it until this guilt feeling goes away. Well guess what I no longer feel guilty. It feels really good to be able to buy myself something.

Initially on I talked about how I volunteered at a nursing home, but I felt I needed to do more. My calling in life is to help people. I now volunteer for Hope for Kids. They work with children who are in the foster care system. I am also going to train to become a foster parent. There are a lot of kids out there that need families. They need someone to love them. Some of them don't even know what's going on. I'm not saying it's easy. They come from jail in and out of homes. They also come from all over the world. Sometimes they come to this organization with nothing. This organization was started by a judge back in 1969. She is an amazing person. With Hope for Kids, I also help out with events or pitch in with whatever else they need. It is the best thing to give back. I believe everyone should take some time from his or her day or week to help someone in need. We all need to pay it forward. It would make this world a much better place. At fifty-one years old, I am beginning to live my life and enjoy it. I can now go to places by myself which I could never do. But I have also made many new friendships. Life gets much easier when you accept the apologies but never forget the pain. The key is to be thankful for all of the experiences, positive and negative. It's taking a step back to say thank you for the lesson. It's realizing that grudges from the past are a waste of today's happiness.

I have never experienced the apologies. I can accept everything else. That's how you learn from the negative and positive lessons in life. Think of where you would be today if you didn't have those lessons. You wouldn't be a happy person. You would be making other people unhappy. You didn't choose to be here. God embedded a seed inside your mother's womb, and you are God's child, whether you accept it or not. You are here for a reason, and that reason you may never know. But you, with God's help, can choose what you want to be. You can be good, or you can be evil.

Don't be afraid to ask for help. There is plenty of help out there today. This is where I am today, telling you my story. I hope that it will help other children who have been in my situation.

ACKNOWLEGEMENTS

Writing this book has been a journey with the help of many different people. I am eternally grateful for the wonderful people in making this project enjoyable and memorable.

Many thanks to some of the greatest friends anyone could have. Thank you to those who have helped me make my dream come true. I am immensely grateful for my two boys, friends and mentors who have influenced my life in an enormous way. I couldn't have done it without you. I am blessed to have such wonderful people in my life. You have encouraged and inspired me to finally finish my destiny.

Today at the age of fifty-one I am standing on my own two feet. My journey takes you to a place of physical and verbal abuse. My Mother who hated her own flesh a blood, beat me day and night. My biological father sexually abused me as a little girl. I was always on the run to somewhere. I would stay at friend's house. I once was put in temporary foster care. I have been raped several times. Throughout my life I had met all the wrong people. Even the men I met were abusive in some way or another. I wound up having three children by three different fathers.

How I fought through mental illness, and my children's challenges along the way. But then something changed. I found peace with God. I now have wonderful friendships. I am helping other children who have been in my situation.

You can find me on my blog @
www.agnesnancyprobst.blogspot.com
I can answer any questions you may have.
Twitter @nancyprobst2
Facebook-Nancy Probst
Email Address- ncgrandma44@aol.com

I would love to hear from you.